Warfare

P R A Y E R

FIVE YEARS AGO I COULD NOT HAVE WRITTEN THIS
book. But around 1990 what seemed like a divine
alarm went off, calling the Church worldwide to
serious spiritual warfare on a scale and intensity previously unknown. At that time God put me on the fastest
learning curve I have experienced in 35 years of ministry. I feel compelled to share what I am learning in
this book.

I believe that through this book God can change
you and your church, putting you on the front lines of
the greatest forward thrust of world evangelization in
2,000 years of Christian history.

C. Peter Wagner

WARFARE PRAYER

C. PETER WAGNER

MONARCH
Tunbridge Wells

First published in the USA by
Regal Books, a division of GL Publications, Ventura, California

First British edition 1992
Reprinted 1993

ISBN 1 85424 173 7

British Library Cataloguing in Publication Data
A catalogue record for this book is available from the British Library

Rights for publishing this book in other languages are contracted by
Gospel Literature International (GLINT). GLINT also provides
technical help for the adaptation, translation, and publishing of Bible
study resources and books in scores of languages worldwide. For
further, information, contact GLINT, Post Office Box 488,
Rosemead, California, 91770, U.S.A., or the publisher.

Production and printing in England for
MONARCH PUBLICATIONS LTD
PO Box 163, Tunbridge Wells, Kent TN3 0NZ
Nuprint Ltd, Station Road, Harpenden, Herts AL5 4SE.

Lovingly dedicated to the Potter family
Karen and Curt
Christopher, Phillip and Jennifer

Contents

WARFARE PRAYER

WARFARE PRAYER

Introduction

WARFARE PRAYER

A WAVE OF INTEREST IN THE SUPERNATURAL AND IN CHRIS-
tian positions relating to spiritual warfare has been
growing for some years throughout the Christian
world. Books by authors such as Frank Peretti have
stimulated certain audiences while books of other
authors such as Walter Wink have stimulated other audiences. "Breakthroughs" led by Larry Lea and spiritual
warfare conferences led by John Wimber attract thousands. Some theological seminaries are introducing
courses on spirituality and power encounter, and healing and deliverance. A partial list of these appears in
my book, *Wrestling with Dark Angels* (Regal Books).

I personally began tuning in to this new emphasis
around 1980 when I began research on the spiritual
dimensions of church growth. I spent several years
looking into the influence of supernatural signs and
wonders on the growth of churches and compiled my
findings in the book, *How to Have a Healing Ministry*
(Regal Books). Then in 1987 I began researching prayer.

After spending considerable time building a personal library and some bibliographies on prayer, I discovered three areas in the field that seemed important to me, and that are not adequately covered in research, writing and teaching. They are: (1) strategic-level intercession, (2) intercession for Christian leaders, and (3) the relationship of prayer to the growth of the local church. I am dedicating several years to concentrate on these three areas.

One of the outcomes of my search has been the projection of a trilogy of books on prayer, one on each of the three subjects. This book is the first, dealing with strategic-level spiritual warfare and the warfare prayer necessary to engage in it.

Many new books are coming out on spiritual warfare, but none of them so far has attempted to survey the field and draw broadly from theologians, biblical scholars, current authors and practitioners. A glance through the footnotes and the index of this book will indicate the spectrum of authorities I have consulted. I am grateful to them all. I certainly could not have written a very substantial book on my knowledge and experiences alone.

Certain subjects handled in some depth in this book have so far not found their way into print. I have included more biblical material here than I have found in any other book, partly because many are questioning whether there is biblical warrant for strategic-level spiritual warfare at all. The concepts of spiritual territoriality and the naming of the powers have received considerable attention here. Holiness is frequently mentioned in the other books, but rarely is it analyzed in the depth I believe is required for effective warfare prayer. Many other subjects I deal with have also been mentioned by others, but each of us brings a particular insight that adds to our collective knowledge.

All this may sound as though you have a scholarly treatise in your hands. I hope it has scholarly integrity, but each chapter is full of lively stories and anecdotes from the United States and other parts of the world, especially Argentina. I am a theoretician, but I am one of those who has a bias toward theories that work. My principal laboratory for testing these theories has been Argentina, so you will read of many incidents that happened there. Some are serious and tragic such as the death of a witch. Some are humorous such as the "Demon of Keys."

My awareness of the potential strategic-level spiritual warfare has for effective evangelism was first sparked by Pastor Omar Cabrera of Argentina. His "Vision of the Future" is listed as one of the world's ten largest churches. When I visited him in 1985, he told me his personal experience of identifying and binding the territorial spirits controlling cities in which he was pioneering new works. I am deeply indebted to Omar and his wife, Marfa, for the inspiration and support they have given me in this project.

I was fascinated to read a recent letter from Bernie May, the director of Wycliffe Bible Translators. My interest was piqued, partially because Wycliffe as an organization has been one which up to now has not particularly stressed strategic-level spiritual warfare, although many of their field translators and staff have been involved from time to time. But this comes from the head office.

Bernie May tells of a veteran translator who visited his office and, among other things, said, "I have two major goals while I'm home. One, I need to learn as much as I can about spiritual warfare. Our struggle out there is not against the climate, the malaria, or the false religions. Our struggle is against the principalities, against the powers, against the world rulers of this present darkness, against the spiritual hosts of wickedness in the heavenly places of Ephesians 6:12."

He went on. "My other goal," he said, "is to find some more people who will stand with us in prayer. The only way we are going to break through the spiritual darkness in that land is by prayer. I need intercessors to stand with me."

Needless to say, I was excited to find the top two agenda items of this missionary were the subjects of the first two books in the trilogy on prayer that I am writing.

But I was even more excited when Bernie May himself wrote, "Like my friend from Asia, I, too, need to know about spiritual warfare. And I need people to stand with me in prayer."

I am convinced this is what the Spirit is saying, not only to Wycliffe Bible Translators, but to the churches throughout the nations of the world. My prayer is that those who are hearing what the Spirit is saying will find this book an instrument in God's hands to help them draw closer to Him and to open themselves in a new way to powerful warfare prayer.

C. Peter Wagner
Fuller Theological Seminary
Pasadena, California

Frontline Warfare

CHAPTER ONE

ARGENTINA IS A GOOD BEGINNING SCENARIO TO explain what warfare prayer is all about.

As I write, I have three current short lists of nations that have a special importance to me:

- Nations at this time experiencing the greatest outpouring of the power of the Spirit of God: China and Argentina.
- Nations highest on my personal ministry agenda: Japan and Argentina.
- Nations of the Third World that now offer specific contributions to Christianity in the Western world: Korea on prayer and Argentina on spiritual warfare.

Since 1990, my wife, Doris, and I have made many ministry trips to Argentina to observe firsthand and participate in what amounts to a laboratory for relating strategic-level spiritual warfare to evangelism. For us, Argentina has been the front line in a highly significant experiment helping us to learn more about the spiritual dimensions of world evangelization.

THREE LEVELS OF SPIRITUAL WARFARE

As I see the world picture unfolding, the year 1990 marked the beginning of a strong upsurge of interest across denominational lines in spiritual warfare, particularly what I like to call strategic-level spiritual warfare.

When all is said and done, there are probably many, many different discernable levels of spiritual warfare. At this point I will suggest three generalized levels for which there is a fairly broad consensus among Christian leaders who are specializing in this type of ministry. I realize that each one of the three will allow for several subdivisions, and that there will also be considerable overlapping around the rather fine lines that separate them. But I have found it helpful to distinguish the following:

1. Ground-level spiritual warfare. This is the ministry of casting out demons. The first time Jesus sent out His 12 disciples, "He gave them power over unclean spirits, to cast them out" (Matt. 10:1). When the 70, whom Jesus sent out in Luke 10, returned from their mission, they said with great joy, "Lord, even the demons are subject to us in Your name" (Luke 10:17). When Philip evangelized Samaria, "unclean spirits, crying with a loud voice, came out of many who were possessed" (Acts 8:7). All these are instances of ground-level spiritual warfare.

Ground-level spiritual warfare is the most common variety we find in the New Testament, and it is the most common variety practiced by Christians today. Groups and individuals involved in "deliverance ministries" by and large are engaged in ground-level spiritual warfare. In modern times we have seen a good bit of this in the United States, particularly among Pentecostals and charismatics, and missionaries of all stripes have brought back stories of it from the mission fields. In parts of the world such as India, most converts in some village churches have been delivered from evil spirits. Throughout lands such as China, Nepal or Mozambique, effective evangelism is all but inconceivable without an accompanying ministry of deliverance.

Most books in Christian bookstores on spiritual warfare deal with ground-level warfare. Although they are relatively new to some of us, deliverance ministries have been going on around us for some time and a good number of Christian leaders, although not nearly enough in my opinion, have accumulated considerable expertise in the field.

2. Occult-level spiritual warfare. It seems evident that we see a kind of demonic power at work through shamans, New Age channelers, occult practitioners, witches and warlocks, satanist priests, fortune-tellers and the like. This is substantially different from the ordinary demon who may cause headaches, marital blowups, drunkenness or scoliosis. When the apostle Paul was in Philippi, a demonized fortune-teller annoyed him for many days until he finally cast the spirit out of her. This apparently was something different from the ordinary demon because the event caused such a political commotion that the missionaries were jailed (see Acts 16:16-24).

Not too many years ago, Christians in the United States were fairly ignorant of this occult-level spiritual activity. Some did not even seem to pay a great deal of attention to Nancy and Ronald Reagan using an astrologer as a consultant for presidential-level decision-making in Washington. The fact that Governor Michael Dukakis had named a woman as official witch of the state of Massachusetts may *not* have been a major reason why evangelicals did not vote for him for president. Few at that time had much information about occult-level spiritual warfare.

Things are changing, however. Word that the number of registered witches in Germany exceeds the number of registered Christian clergy is startling. A missionary to France reports that more French people who are sick consult witch doctors than medical doctors. Hard data are elusive, but in all proba-

---

In a valid sense, Jesus came to destroy the works of the devil, but this was only a means toward the end of seeking and saving that which was lost.

---

bility the most rapidly growing religious movement in America is the New Age. Excellent books such as Russell Chandler's *Understanding the New Age* (Word Inc.), Paul McGuire's *Supernatural Faith in the New Age* (Whitaker House) and *Evangelizing the New Age* (Servant Publications), are raising our level of consciousness and concern about occult-level spiritual warfare. The cover of the April 29, 1991, *Christianity Today* shows demonic power coming to earth from a full moon. Mark I. Bubeck's *The Satanic Revival* (Here's Life Publishers) documents much of what is happening in the United States and offers suggestions for Christian action.

3. Strategic-level spiritual warfare. Here we contend with an even more ominous concentration of demonic power: territorial spirits. In Ephesians Paul writes, "we do not wrestle against flesh and blood, but against principalities, against powers, against the rulers of the darkness of this age, against spiritual hosts of wickedness in the heavenly places" (Eph. 6:12). Nothing in this verse itself indicates that one or more of these categories would necessarily fit the description of territorial spirits, but many, including myself, feel it is highly probable. (I will discuss this issue later in the book.)

A clear biblical account of strategic-level spiritual warfare is found in Revelation 12 where we are told, "war broke out in heaven: Michael and his angels fought against the dragon; and the dragon and his angels fought" (Rev. 12:7). This is something quite different from dealing with the occult or casting out a demon of lust.

Undoubtedly, the single-most influential event that has stimulated interest in strategic-level spiritual warfare among American Christians was the publication of Frank Peretti's two novels, *This Present Darkness* and *Piercing the Darkness* (Crossway Books). Many Christians who had scarcely given thought to the possibility that events shaping human society could have a relationship to struggles among powerful supernatural beings are now openly talking about the likelihood. In fact, even though they know better, many find themselves reading *This Present Darkness* as a documentary rather than as somewhat fanciful fiction.

THE FOCUS OF THIS BOOK

This book is about strategic-level spiritual warfare and the kind of prayer required to address it. Not that it can be totally and cleanly separated from the other two kinds of spiritual warfare. As readers of *This Present Darkness* will readily understand, the three levels are closely interrelated and what happens on one level can and will affect what happens on other levels. In all probability I will find myself crossing the lines from time to time, but the emphasis will be on strategic-level, or some call it cosmic-level, intercession.

I do not believe that we should see spiritual warfare as an end in itself. In a valid sense, Jesus came to destroy the works of the devil (see 1 John. 3:8), but this was only a means toward the end of seeking and saving that which was lost (see Luke 19:10). Jesus mainly wanted to draw human beings back into fellowship with the Father and He was willing to die on the cross so it could be possible. His focus was on people, and the devil was simply one of those obstacles, albeit the most formidable one, standing in the way of human redemption. I see the heart of God as so loving the world that He gave His only begotten Son. For what reason? So that all who believe on Him should not perish but have everlasting life (see John 3:16).

God's highest priority is evangelism, calling out a people who will honor and glorify His name. This is my highest priority as well. I have given over 35 years of active ministry to missions, evangelism and church growth. If I have 10 more years to serve God, I want them to make a difference in the number of souls that are saved around the world. My interest in warfare prayer is directly proportional to its effectiveness in enhancing evangelism.

Which brings me back to Argentina.

ARGENTINA

Evicting the Ruler of Adrogué

The upper-middle-class suburb of Buenos Aires called Adrogué had experienced little effective evangelism. Many had tried, but none had succeeded. Most of the Protestant churches planted in Adrogué had struggled and then closed their doors. It was a graveyard of church planters. One of the survivors was a Baptist church, which after 70 years of attempting to evangelize Adrogué counted only 70 members. More disturbing yet, virtually none of the 70 members were residents of Adrogué proper. No one could remember a single resident of Adrogué being converted.

Pastor Eduardo Lorenzo accepted a call to the church in

1974. He was a dynamic leader who applied church growth principles and in 13 years, to 1987, the church had grown from 70 to 250. Still, few of the members lived in Adrogué.

In 1987 a growth surge began. When I visited the church in 1990, it had passed the 600 mark and they had constructed a new auditorium that could accommodate 2,000. By mid-1991 more than 1,000 attended. Eduardo Lorenzo said to me, "If we do not make 2,000 members by 1993, it will be because we are not trying!"

What happened in 1987? How did mediocre evangelism become effective evangelism?

The answer was the frontline application of strategic-level spiritual warfare. This did not come about quickly or easily. Eduardo Lorenzo, like many of us, had not been trained in spiritual warfare of any kind. Some of his seminary professors considered dealing with the demonic something those Pentecostals might do, but off-limits for respectable Baptists. Coming from this background, it took Lorenzo several years to get to the root of the evangelistic difficulties in Adrogué and begin to understand the spiritual dimensions of the issue.

Face-to-Face with a Demon

It began in the early 1980s when Pastor Lorenzo found himself face-to-face with a demonized woman. Although he felt totally inadequate to attempt it, he rebuked the demon in Jesus' name. It left and the woman was delivered! This did not launch Lorenzo into a regular ministry of deliverance, but it did perk his interest. Just then one of his church members traveled to the United States, learned some things about spiritual warfare, and reported back to the congregation. Lorenzo sponsored two spiritual warfare seminars in his church. One was led by Edward Murphy of Overseas Crusades and the other by John White, the well-known Christian psychiatrist and author from

Canada. The process of retooling a congregation was underway.

Soon afterward the battle began in earnest: The enemy attempted infiltration. A woman who feigned conversion to Christ was discovered to be an undercover agent of the demonic forces over Adrogué. Demons began to manifest openly in church services. Satan was counterattacking and attempting to intimidate the believers. Eduardo Lorenzo says, "Satan was happy if he could keep that little Baptist church on its merry-go-round. He had effectively blinded the minds of the unsaved in Adrogué to the gospel. Through the years several other churches had been destroyed. Now we ourselves were under direct attack."

Through a prolonged process of prayer, ministry and discernment, Lorenzo and his leaders finally identified the chief demonic principality over Adrogué. They even discovered the name of this territorial spirit. Sensing God's timing for the final battle, they recruited a team of 35 or 40 church members who agreed to spend Monday through Friday of a certain week in prayer and fasting. On the Friday night 200 believers, almost the entire congregation, joined together for the strategic-level intercession. They took authority over the principality over the city and the lesser demonic forces.

At 11:45 that evening, they collectively felt something break in the spiritual realm. They knew the battle was over. The evil spirit had left, and the church began to grow. Not only did the membership triple in a short period of time, but now 40 percent of the church members are from Adrogué itself.

The year of the victory was 1987!

Argentina's Decline

In all probability, what happened in Adrogué in 1987 would not have happened in 1977, ten years earlier. Of all the nations in Latin America, Argentina, along with a few others such as

Uruguay and Venezuela, had not seen the rapid growth of Protestant or evangelical churches so characteristic of the continent as a whole. Argentines had been widely known as indifferent or resistant to the gospel. With the exception of the extraordinary impact of the Tommy Hicks evangelistic crusade in the early 1950s, the evangelical movement in Argentina had been relatively stagnant.

A dramatic change came with the Falkland Islands war against Great Britain in 1982 when Argentina tried unsuccessfully to occupy the Malvinas Islands, as Argentines call them. The British victory caused a radical change in Argentine social psychology. Argentines had gained the unenviable international reputation of being the proudest people in Latin America, but their national pride was shattered. Many became bitter. The church had failed them, the military had failed them, Peronism had failed them. They were ready to try something new!

The basis for Argentine pride had been seriously eroding well before 1982. Once the world's tenth strongest economic power and boasting a standard of living higher than that of southern Europe, Argentina was justly considered by many as the jewel of South America. Juan Domingo Perón was flying high as their political leader through much of the 1950s and 1960s. But as his influence began to wane in the early 1970s, Perón linked up with a powerful occult practitioner, José López Rega, known popularly as *el brujo* (the warlock). López Rega served under Perón as social welfare minister, and after Perón's death in 1974 he became the chief advisor to his third wife, Isabel Perón, during her two years as president. He succeeded in erecting a public monument to witchcraft (since dismantled), and is said by many to have openly cursed the nation when he lost power with the military coup of 1976.

The wicked principalities and powers over Argentina were, quite obviously, having a field day. Their mission is to steal, kill and destroy, and they were doing all that and more to one of the finest countries of the world.

Spiritism, principally from Brazil, began to flood the nation. Under the military rulers, thousands, some say tens of thousands, of political suspects "disappeared" forever, the bodies of many recently being uncovered in remote mass graves. Once the world's tenth strongest economic power, Argentina now finds itself tenth from the bottom by some measurements.

Little wonder the nation is now ripe for the gospel message. True enough, in such a spiritual vacuum and surrounded by such social misery, almost any change is seen by many as a change for the better. The power of witchcraft continues to escalate. Occult artifacts are displayed in store windows on every other block. False cults such as Mormonism are experiencing rapid growth. A huge ornate Mormon temple dominates the highway leading from the Ezeiza airport to Buenos Aires. According to *Somos* magazine, Carlos Menem, Argentina's president at this writing, consults regularly with a "personal witch" named Ilda Evelia, whom he has retained for 28 years. *Somos* also quotes a high government official, "The truth of the matter is that the majority of us consult witches. And we do it very frequently."

Spiritual Vitality

Although much of Argentina is still struggling in the grips of the rulers of darkness, the light of the gospel of Christ is bursting forth as never before. God is raising up a company of world-class Argentine leaders He is using to open the "eyes [of the Argentines] and to turn them from darkness to light, and from the power of Satan to God, that they may receive forgiveness of sins and an inheritance among those who are sanctified by faith in Me" (Acts 26:18).

J. Philip Hogan, until recently executive director of the Division of Foreign Missions of the Assemblies of God, knows as well as anyone what God is doing in the world. His international travels have taken him to Argentina many times over many years. He is amazed at what he now sees in Argentina. Hogan says, "Argentina is in the throes of an absolute sovereign revival unheard of in the history of that country. I know of churches where they have taken the seats out so they can pack more people in."[1]

Edgardo Silvoso of Harvest Evangelism, one of the leading experts on the Christian movement in Argentina, said in 1987, "The church in Argentina has grown more in the last four years than in the previous one hundred."[2]

Silvoso's "four years" date back to 1984 when evangelist Carlos Annacondia conducted his first large evangelistic crusade in the city of La Plata. Many observers use this as the beginning date of the current outpouring of spiritual vitality in Argentina.

Carlos Annacondia

Carlos Annacondia was a committed Christian owner of a prosperous nuts and bolts factory in Quilmes on the outskirts of Buenos Aires when God called him into evangelistic ministry. It was probably no mere coincidence that the day he launched his first public crusade was the day the British sank the Argentine battleship *General Belgrano* in the 1982 Falkland Islands War. Carlos was 37 years old and the father of 8 children at the time.

After observing the ministry of Carlos Annacondia both at a distance and first hand, I am prepared to offer a hypothesis. Although some other likely contenders may be Reinhard Bonnke or Billy Graham, my guess is that Annacondia may well turn out to be the most effective crusade evangelist of all time. More than any other evangelist I have studied, Annacondia's ministry seems to be an instrument for increasing the growth rate of participating churches.

In La Plata, for example, the Assemblies of God Church of the Diagonal, pastored by Alberto Scataglini, grew from 500 to more than 2,500 in 3 years following Annacondia's crusade. They have held their Sunday services in a leased basketball stadium ever since because their sanctuary could not hold all the attenders. The neighboring Los Olivos Baptist Church pastored by Alberto Prokopchuk grew from 200 members to more than 1,600 in the same period.

On a recent visit to Argentina I worked with pastors of four cities. Without any leading questions on my part, in each of the four cities I heard Christian leaders in a matter-of-fact way refer to recent trends in their cities as "before Annacondia" and "after Annacondia." In more than 20 years of studying urban crusade evangelism, I have never heard such consistent testimonials of the ministry of a single evangelist across the board. Pastor Alberto Scataglini, the principal host of Annacondia's milestone La Plata crusade, says, "He transmits his ministry. It's not just one person; wherever he goes, he seems to transmit the same anointing to other people. And that was very different from any other evangelist we had here. Before, the evangelist would come and when he left the revival was over; the power was gone."[3]

WARFARE PRAYER

What is Carlos Annacondia doing that other urban crusade evangelists do not usually do? I believe it is warfare prayer. My friend Edgardo Silvoso agrees.

Edgardo Silvoso says that Annacondia and the other prominent Argentine evangelists "incorporate into their evangelistic work a new emphasis on spiritual warfare—the challenging of the principalities and powers, and the proclamation of the gospel not only to the people but to the spiritual jailers who held the people captive." Prayer is the chief variable, according to Silvoso. "Evangelists begin to pray over cities before proclaiming the gospel there. Only after they sense that spiritual powers over the region have been bound will they begin to preach."[4]

A permanent fixture of Annacondia's crusades is what has to be one of the most sophisticated and massive deliverance ministries anywhere. Under the direction of Pablo Bottari, a wise, mature and gifted servant of God, literally thousands of individ-

---

I do not see warfare prayer as an end in itself....My chief interest is warfare prayer that helps bring about effective evangelism.

---

uals are delivered from demons each of the 30 to 50 consecutive nights of a crusade. The 150-foot deliverance tent, erected behind the open-air speaker's platform, is in operation from 8:00 P.M. to 4:00 A.M. each night. Annacondia calls it the "spiritual intensive care unit." Scores of teams whom Bottari has trained in deliverance prayer do the actual hands-on ministry.

I have never observed a crusade evangelist who is as publicly aggressive in confronting evil spirits as Annacondia. With a high-volume, high-energy, prolonged challenge, he actually taunts the spirits until they manifest in one way or another. To the uninitiated, the scenario in the vacant city lot where he holds his crusades might appear to be total confusion. But to the skilled, experienced members of Annacondia's 31 crusade ministry teams, it is just another evening of frontline warfare prayer in which the power of Jesus Christ over the demonic forces is displayed for all to see.

And the power of the meetings is awesome. Many miraculous healings occur. For example, so many dental miracles occur—teeth filled, new teeth and defective bridges replaced by whole teeth—that only those who have had more than two teeth filled are allowed to take the time to give a public testimony. On one occasion, a dwarf was reported to grow over 15 inches taller.

Unsuspecting pedestrians passing by the crusade meetings have been known to fall down under the power of the Holy Spirit. In the city of Santiago del Estero, a local priest decided to oppose the crusade by invading the area with a religious procession. When they arrived, the four strong men carrying the statue of the priest's favorite virgin all fell to the ground under the power of the Spirit and the statue shattered into a thousand pieces. Two of the men spent the night in the hospital and the other two in Annacondia's deliverance tent!

This is warfare prayer in action. Spirit-directed prayer opens the way for the blessings of the Kingdom of God to come upon the earth with healings, deliverances, salvation, holiness, compassion for the poor and oppressed, and the fruit of the Spirit. Above all, God is glorified, worshiped and praised.

DRAWING THE BATTLE LINES

As I have said before, I do not see warfare prayer as an end in itself. I am a very pragmatic person in the sense that the theories I like best are the ones that work. My chief interest is warfare prayer that helps bring about effective evangelism such as in the ministry of Carlos Annacondia. My wife, Doris, and I were privileged to participate in a real-life experiment in the relationship of spiritual warfare to evangelism in the Argentine city of Resistencia.

Edgardo Silvoso is a world-class evangelistic strategist. Years ago, God called him to evangelistic ministry in his native land of Argentina. But after some time he became dissatisfied, wondering if the fruit he saw in decisions for Christ was truly the fruit that endures. Silvoso had read a research, which found that in the average city-wide evangelistic crusade, only 3 to 16 percent of those who make first-time decisions ever end up in the cooperating churches. And very few, if any, churches report a noticeable increase in their growth rate after the crusade. He began to suspect there must be a better way to evangelize.

Ed Silvoso studied church growth at Fuller Seminary and developed a radically different city-wide evangelistic strategy, which he called *Plan Rosario* because he was going to test it in the city of Rosario, Argentina. He teamed up with his brother-in-law, Luis Palau, and tried the experiment in 1976. Instead of 3 to 16 percent, a full 47 percent of those making first-time decisions were assimilated into the churches. This is not the place to go into detail on the evangelistic strategy, but the major innovations had to do with setting goals for disciples, rather than decisions, and planting new churches.[5] Two years later Silvoso and Palau repeated the effort in Uruguay and recorded 54 percent assimilation.

Then Edgardo Silvoso contracted a rare, fatal illness, myesthenia gravis. He was given a maximum of two years to live. That was when he founded his current ministry, Harvest Evangelism, which maintains offices both in Buenos Aires, Argentina, and in San Jose, California. God brought intercessors into his life, and through prayer he was miraculously healed. The whole episode brought Ed and his wife, Ruth, into a closer relationship with God than they had ever had before, and introduced them to a hitherto underemphasized tool for evangelism: spiritual warfare!

The Fall of Merigildo
As a test case, Silvoso drew a circle with a 100-mile radius around his hometown of San Nicolás where he was establishing his Harvest Evangelism training center. He discovered that within that circle were 109 towns and villages with no evan-

gelical church. Research showed that a powerful warlock, Merigildo, had applied supernatural occult power to the area to keep out the gospel. Silvoso gathered Christian leaders, Pentecostal and non-Pentecostal, together for serious warfare prayer. They took dominion over the area in the name of Jesus. Silvoso said, "We served the disciples of Merigildo and the rulers of darkness over them an eviction notice sealed with the blood of Jesus Christ." They sensed the power was broken. Just recently I received a report from Silvoso that all 109 towns now have an evangelical church!

Plan Resistencia

After the Merigildo experience, the city of Resistencia in the northern Argentina province of Chaco came to Silvoso's attention. The revival so prevalent in many parts of Argentina had seemed to bypass Resistencia. Resistencia is Spanish for "resistance." Although the name originally had military connotations, the city turned out to be spiritually resistant as well. As of the beginning of 1990, fewer than 6,000 of its 400,000 population were evangelical believers, a mere 1.5 percent.

In 1989, Silvoso had initiated a three-year *Plan Resistencia* aimed at significant, measurable evangelism. He based it not only on state-of-the-art church growth techniques, but even more importantly on the spiritual warfare he had been learning about. Silvoso discerned two major demonic strongholds over the evangelical community in Resistencia, a spirit of disunity and a spirit of apathy toward the lost. He moved members of his Harvest Evangelism team into Resistencia and for over a year laid a foundation of prayer, spiritual warfare and leadership training.

By April of 1990 the tide had turned. Almost all the pastors were united and in agreement with the Plan Resistencia. Christian people had begun witnessing and speaking of their neighbors as those who were "not yet believers." Disunity and apathy had been defeated by the power of God.

In April 1990, Ed Silvoso invited my wife, Doris, and me to visit Resistencia and train leaders in church growth principles. While I was training leaders, Doris was taking the spiritual temperature of the city. What she discovered alarmed her. It became obvious that the believers had meager knowledge about strategic-level spiritual warfare and warfare prayer. Unless this could be changed, the chances of a significant evangelistic impact were slim. She sensed that God wanted to see it changed.

Calling the Generals

My wife, Doris, and Ed Silvoso agreed to call in one of the leading experts in warfare prayer, our friend Cindy Jacobs of Generals of Intercession. Cindy and Doris made three more visits to Argentina in 1990. The question in my mind was whether intentional strategic-level spiritual warfare could actually make a measurable difference in evangelizing Resistencia.

In June, Cindy taught two intensive seminars on warfare prayer to several hundred pastors, intercessors and other Christian leaders first in Buenos Aires and then in Resistencia. Marfa Cabrera, who with her husband, Omar, were precursors of the Argentine revival, teamed with Cindy as her interpreter. The impact was electric. Not only did the Argentine leaders want to know about strategic-level intercession, but they wanted to see it done and they wanted to do it. Now!

Sensing the direction of God, Cindy invited those who felt a special call of God and who had their lives in order to assemble the next morning in the city. A group of 80 showed up and marched into the central Plaza de Mayo of Buenos Aires for five hours of intense battle against the spiritual forces of wickedness in heavenly places. Eduardo Lorenzo, pastor of the

Baptist Church in Adrogué and director of Harvest Evangelism in Argentina, led the small army of intercessors.

Among other things, the group sensed a spirit of witchcraft and a spirit of death in the Ministry of Social Welfare building where Perón's notorious warlock, José López Rega, had maintained his office. Cindy felt that before going to Resistencia, it was necessary to serve notice of the coming of the Kingdom of God to any evil powers that might have had national influence.

When the group left the plaza, they felt a sense of victory. The principalities and powers had *not* been destroyed, but warfare prayer had in some measure begun to weaken the evil hold they were exerting on Argentina.

Arriving in Resistencia, Cindy, Doris, Marfa, Eduardo and the others found that the names of the spirits ruling over that city had been known by the people for generations. San La Muerte, the spirit of death, was perhaps the most powerful. A large number of citizens of Resistencia were so devoted to San La Muerte that they had tiny bone images of his idol surgically implanted under their skin or under their nipples, believing the false promise that this will assure them of a "good death." It is hard to imagine the degree of emptiness and despair that had penetrated the city.

Other spirits of almost equal rank turned out to be Pombero, a spirit of division who brought terror, especially to children during the siesta time and at night; Curupí, a spirit of sexual perversion and incest whose image was characterized by a ridiculously long male organ; the Queen of Heaven, a religious spirit, who had perverted the true character of the traditional church; and the spirit of Freemasonry, a cleverly disguised form of occult power. Apparently coordinating their activities was a principality of divination or witchcraft, represented by a snake.

Surprisingly, the images of these spirits and their activities were clearly depicted on several large folk art murals in the central plaza of the city. After Cindy taught a day-long seminar on warfare prayer to pastors, intercessors, the Harvest Evangelism team and others, a group of around 70 felt led to go to the plaza and engage in frontline warfare. After collectively praying, repenting and confessing the sins represented by these evil principalities and powers, they engaged the spirits in five hours of spiritual battle. Only then did God give them an assurance in their spirits that they had broken through. When it was over, they lifted their voices together in praise and victory.

Fruit That Endures

What happened?

The Harvest Evangelism Plan Resistencia proceeded as scheduled with city-wide evangelistic events in August and October 1990. Cindy and Doris visited twice more. Edgardo Silvoso reports that the growth graphs of the churches in Resistencia took a decided turn upward beginning in April when the group prayed in the plaza. In one public event, 250 people were baptized in portable pools. Crowds of almost 17,000 packed into an open field for evangelistic meetings where objects used in occult rituals and witchcraft were burned in a 55-gallon drum each night. The mayor of the city was reported to have made a profession of faith in Christ. Hundreds were healed physically and delivered from demons. At least 18 new churches were started.

Most significant of all, the evangelical population of Resistencia virtually doubled in the calendar year of 1990. Reports like this indicate that warfare prayer undoubtedly had some direct effect on the evangelistic fruit.

Perhaps a weakening sign of the territorial spirits over Resistencia was the tragic fate of the high priestess of the cult of San La Muerte, the spirit of death. Two weeks before the massive evangelistic thrust began in October, her bed caught fire. For some reason the flames seemed to be selective. They consumed only the mattress, the woman, and her statue of San La Muerte!

San La Muerte kept his promise of granting his followers a good death in the manner that would be expected of the father of lies!

■ REFLECTION QUESTIONS ■

1. Look back at the description of the three levels of spiritual warfare (pp. 16-19). Name examples of each that you have personally experienced or heard about.
2. Do you agree that "we should not see spiritual warfare as an end in itself"? Discuss your opinion.
3. When the territorial spirit was cast out of Androgué, Eduardo Lorenzo had learned its name. How important do you think it is that names be revealed?
4. Talk about Carlos Annacondia's crusades. How would a crusade like that go over in your city?
5. What do you think actually happened in the heavenlies as a result of the five-hour spiritual battle in the plaza of Resistencia?

Notes

1. Stephen Strang, "Revival Surges in Argentina," *Charisma and Christian Life*, April 1989, p. 34.
2. Edgardo Silvoso, "Prayer Power in Argentina," *Engaging the Enemy*, C. Peter Wagner, ed., (Ventura, CA: Regal Books, 1991), p. 110.
3. Daniel E. Wray, "¡Revivé Argentina!" *Eternity*, July/August 1987, p. 22.
4. Edgardo Silvoso, "Argentina: Battleground of the Spirit," *World Christian*, October 1989, p. 16.
5. For more information on the evangelistic principles used by Silvoso in the *Plan Rosario*, see C. Peter Wagner, *Strategies for Church Growth* (Ventura, CA: Regal Books, 1987), p. 149.

The Real Battle Is Spiritual

CHAPTER TWO

WARFARE PRAYER, AS I HAVE BEEN DESCRIBING IT, IS A new concept to the great majority of American Christians. Many are beginning to ask whether, given their traditions and training, it could ever be integrated into their ministry. But Americans are not alone. Even Argentine pastors struggle with some of the same theological and practical issues.

LEARNING THE LESSON

I greatly enjoyed talking to Pastor Alberto Prokopchuk of the Los Olivos Baptist Church in the city of La Plata, Argentina, because I could identify so closely with his background. His traditional Baptist ministerial training had not included a course in Spiritual Warfare 101. His ministry at Los Olivos Baptist was not much different from what we observe in so many typical churches in our American cities: good, solid Bible teaching ministry; a relatively high moral standard; the fruit of the Spirit manifested to a reasonable degree and church members who pray, tithe, attend services, and witness to their neighbors when the opportunity presents itself.

All this, and no growth!

Under Alberto's ministry, the Los Olivos church had been stalled at 30 members for many years.

Then Carlos Annacondia came to La Plata to conduct a crusade. Alberto and Los Olivos Baptist cooperated with the crusade. As they attended meetings night after night, they began learning about warfare prayer by observing Annacondia. And they were deeply impressed with the results, not only the thousands who were personally healed and delivered from evil spirits, but even more so the 50,000 who made public decisions to follow Christ. Nothing even close to this had been seen previously in La Plata.

Watching Annacondia and his team conduct the crusade was one thing—carrying this type of ministry over to a traditional Baptist church was something else. One thing Baptists did know how to do, however, was to evangelize. So the lay leaders of Los Olivos approached Pastor Alberto and said, "Let's have an evangelistic crusade in our own church."

Alberto wasn't ready for that. "I don't have the gift of evangelist," he replied. "Should we invite an outside evangelist?"

"No," his leaders said. "Let's make a deal. You preach the crusade and we will pray that God gives you the gift of evangelist."

Alberto, possibly in a weak moment, agreed. They organized the crusade and held the first service. Alberto preached an evangelistic message and gave the invitation. No response!

As he was agonizing to himself over this apparent lack of power, Alberto seemed to hear an inner voice saying to him,

"Try it the way Annacondia does it!" In semi-desperation, he decided to go for broke and give it a try. He prayed a strong warfare prayer and directly rebuked the spirits as he had seen Carlos Annacondia do so many times. When he had bound the spirits with the authority that Jesus Christ had given him, he gave the invitation once again. This time more than 15 people sprang out of their seats and actually came running to the front to receive Christ as their Savior and Lord!

Los Olivos Baptist Church has grown from its 30 members

I believe God wants us to do a better job of evangelizing our nation in the years to come. And we will do it, in my opinion, to the degree we understand that the real battle is spiritual.

to more than 900. But that is not all. Prokopchuk has started satellite congregations in other parts of the city with an additional 2,100 members. His goal for his church with its satellite network is 20,000 members by the year 2000. Needless to say, Alberto has been "doing it like Annacondia" ever since.

THE REAL BATTLE

The basic lesson Alberto Prokopchuk learned was that the real battle for effective evangelism is a spiritual battle. He learned it in his way; others of us are learning it in our own way.

The Church Growth Movement, which I represent, has been blessed by God and has been used to stimulate fundamental changes both in local church ministry and in world evange-

lization. The movement began in 1955, and for the first 25 years
or so under the inspiration of its founder, Donald McGavran,
worked on developing the radical new technological aspects of
church growth and evangelism, which have been so widely
acclaimed.

Around 1980, a few of us started to explore what some of
the spiritual dimensions of church growth might look like. This
is not to say that any of the technology is now regarded as bad
or that the spiritual will substitute for the technological. No.
The technological has been extremely helpful to churches and
missions and we continue to work vigorously to improve and
update it.

What we have discovered, however, is that all the evangelistic technology in the world will have only a minimal effect
unless the spiritual battle is won. It is like a brand new automobile with all the latest engineering. It may be beautiful and
perfectly constructed, but it will do nothing until gasoline is
pumped into the tank. The same thing applies to spiritual
power in evangelism and church growth.

To illustrate, look at the decade of the 1980s in America.
This was a decade of the mushrooming of some of the largest
churches the nation has ever seen. Almost every metropolitan
area now has one or more megachurches it did not have previously. Church growth seminars and evangelistic resources
have multiplied. Private Christian schools and the Christian use
of the media increased dramatically. On the surface it looked
like Christianity was making great progress in the nation. But
statistics paint another picture. At the end of the decade church
attendance was the same as at the beginning, and Protestant
church membership had decreased.

I believe God wants us to do a better job of evangelizing
our nation in the years to come. And we will do it, in my opinion, to the degree we understand that the real battle is spiritual.

LEARNING ABOUT THE BATTLE

Around 1980, I began sensing from God that I needed to concentrate on the spiritual dimensions of church growth. Because of my close friendship with John Wimber, who at the time was being called "Mr. Signs and Wonders" by some, I knew that power evangelism would be the first item on my new agenda. I also sensed that after this, prayer would be my next agenda item although, I must admit, at the time I had no clue how prayer might relate to effective evangelism.

I shared the research I had done on signs and wonders in my book *How to Have a Healing Ministry* (Regal Books), which was published in 1988. A year earlier, in 1987, I began to seriously research and teach on prayer. But not until the great Lausanne Congress on World Evangelization in Manila, in the summer of 1989, did I fully learn about the real battle.

Although I didn't know that much about it, by 1989 I had at least begun to realize two things: (1) Evangelism would work better when accompanied by serious prayer; and (2) throughout the Body of Christ, God had gifted, called and anointed certain individuals who were unusually powerful in the ministry of intercession.

I was in a position to integrate these new insights with the Lausanne II Congress because I happened to be a member of the international Lausanne Committee, which was sponsoring the congress.

As I prayed about relating intercession to evangelism, God impressed me with the thought of attempting to identify 30 to 50 of these gifted, world-class intercessors and challenging them to go to Manila at their own expense, bypass the established participant selection process, put up in the Philippine Plaza Hotel across the street from the Convention Center where the congress was to be held, and pray together 24 hours a day throughout the congress. The Lausanne leaders agreed, and I asked Ben Jennings of Campus Crusade's Great Commission Prayer Crusade to organize and lead it. Ben did a magnificent job, and 50 intercessors showed up, fulfilling our highest expectations.

Through the Manila intercession team God gave us what I like to call a "living parable," to show us clearly what the underlying issues for world evangelization really are. Before I describe the living parable, one more crucial factor needs to be explained.

THE THREEFOLD CORD

In the spring of 1989, I began learning about another spiritual dimension relating to evangelism: personal prophecy. I will not go into detail here how individuals such as John Wimber, Cindy Jacobs and Paul Cain helped open this new area of understanding to me except that at the beginning I was somewhat skeptical, but I now believe that the prophetic is a valid and significant ministry in these days.

Early in the summer of 1989 John Wimber told me that Dick Mills would telephone me with a prophecy and he recommended I pay close attention to it. To my embarrassment, I had never heard of Dick Mills but John described him as one of the most respected prophets in America with a well-tested track record. I subsequently learned from Cindy Jacobs, who knew Dick Mills well, that telephoning strangers was contrary to his usual practice. Coincidentally, Cindy happened to be our houseguest the day Dick Mills called my home.

I will not relate the prophecy in detail here, but the item of the living parable in Manila was a prophetic application of Ecclesiastes 4:12 to my ministry: "A threefold cord is not quickly broken." Dick said he felt God was calling me to serve as a catalyst to help bring together three cords that He desired to weave into a pattern to accomplish His purposes in the years to come. The three cords are the *conservative evangelicals,* the *charismatics* and the *conscientious liberals.*

Lausanne II was to play a significant role in bringing together the first two cords. Although Lausanne I in Switzerland in 1974 included only token participation by Pentecostals and charismatics, in Lausanne II, fifteen years later, they were quite prominent. Some said that by looking at the number of raised hands in the plenary sessions, it appeared the majority of participants might well have been charismatic.

It turned out that about half of those who gathered for the intercession team in Manila were conservative evangelicals and about half were Pentecostals or charismatics. I found out later that since this was the first time these two groups had mixed at this level, a variety of thoughts were going through their minds. The charismatics were saying to themselves, "I wonder if these evangelicals really know how to pray and get in touch with God." The evangelicals were saying, "I wonder if these charismatics are going to shout and scream and roll around the floor."

But much to the delight of all concerned, they found that when they began to pray together there was no discernible difference at all. When they entered the throne room of God together they found themselves saying the same things and hearing the same things. The evangelicals were encouraging the charismatics and the charismatics were encouraging the evangelicals. Two of God's cords were coming together.

THE LIVING PARABLE

One of the most dramatic visible signs I have seen from God occurred during the first evening the Lausanne intercession team met in the prayer suite of the Philippine Plaza Hotel. On the eve of the greatest international convocation on evangelization yet held, God gave us a living parable to show us once and for all that the real battle for evangelization is spiritual.

The 50 intercessors sat around the large hotel room in a circle. They had come from 12 nations of the world, the greatest number coming from North America. Ten of the intercessors were Filipinos and Filipinas. Although my wife, Doris, and I are not intercessors, we were invited to participate in the prayer room activities because we happened to be the originators of the idea.

Naturally, the first item of business was to introduce ourselves. As we got a little more than halfway around the circle, a Filipina named Juana Francisco, a woman in her late 50s, introduced herself and told of the ministry of intercession she had exercised for many years. Two or three minutes later, while someone else was speaking, Juana Francisco suffered what we learned later was a critical attack of asthma. She screamed, lost color in her face, and began loudly gasping for breath. A wave of panic went through the room.

Two men took Juana by the arms and half carried her out the door into the hotel corridor. Right across the hall was the room occupied by Bill and Vonette Bright of Campus Crusade, and they managed to get her onto Bill Bright's bed. Fortunately, one of the Filipina intercessors was a medical doctor, so she went out with Juana to attend her. Having the comforting knowledge that she was under medical care, two or three intercessors prayed for her healing, and we continued the introductions.

We had almost completed the circle of introductions when someone burst in the door and shouted, "Who has an automobile? This is an emergency! We must get her to the hospital! The doctor says she is dying!"

Immediately two women jumped out of their chairs and hurried out the other door into the hotel corridor. These women had not known each other well before. One, Mary Lance Sisk, is known as an evangelical. She is a Presbyterian from Charlotte, North Carolina, and has served for years as the personal intercessor for Leighton Ford, the president of the Lausanne Movement and the highest official of the congress. The other was Cindy Jacobs, whom I have mentioned previously. Cindy is a known independent charismatic.

The Voodoo Spirit

Once in the corridor, Mary Lance and Cindy made eye contact and knew at once in the Spirit that they had received the same message from God. God told them both that Juana Francisco's attack was due to the invasion of a voodoo spirit. Philippine voodoo had been spoken against the group and God had pulled back the protection enough to let the afflicting spirit reach the intercessor, much as He had allowed the enemy access to Job in yesteryear. In a matter of seconds, Mary Lance and Cindy grasped hands, agreed in the Spirit, prayed a warfare prayer, and broke the power of the demon in the name of Jesus.

Just at that time, Bill Bright, who knew nothing of what had happened, got off the elevator and went to his room. There on his bed was this strange Filipina woman gasping for breath in a life-threatening situation. His reflex action as a Christian was to lay on hands and pray for her healing, which he did just at the time Mary Lance and Cindy were breaking the curse. Juana Francisco opened her eyes, began breathing normally, and the crisis was over!

By that time Doris and I were out in the corridor. Bill Bright walked out of his room, came over to us, and said with no little emotion in his voice, "We have a lot of power! We should use it more often!"

What Is God Showing Us?

God's purpose behind parables, in this case a living parable, is to teach His people an important lesson. As I analyze this event, the interpretation is clear. Although these 4,500 hand-picked Christian leaders from almost 200 nations of the world gathered at Lausanne II in Manila to strategize the evangelization of the 3 billion people who do not yet know Jesus Christ as Lord and Savior, God wanted them all to know the real nature of their task. I see three major lessons from the parable:

1. World evangelization is a matter of life and death. Medically speaking, Juana Francisco was on the verge of death. Spiritually speaking, 3 billion people in the world are on the verge of an even more terrible death—eternal death in hell. Had Juana Francisco died, she would have gone to heaven. The evangelistic crisis facing God's people is much more serious than was the brief crisis in the Philippine Plaza Hotel because if unbelievers die they do not go to heaven.

2. The key to world evangelization is hearing God and obeying what we hear. Mary Lance Sisk and Cindy Jacobs both received an immediate revelation from God. As seasoned intercessors they were accustomed to this, so it did not take them by surprise. The fact that they had both heard the same word at the same time confirmed to each that they were hearing correctly.

But they also knew that hearing God was only the first step. The second was having the courage to obey Him no matter what. They knew God wanted the curse broken, so they went into action, again doing what they had each done many times before. They took authority in the name of Jesus and neither one had any doubt that at that instant the battle had been won.

3. God is going to use the whole Body of Christ to complete the task of world evangelization. The evangelicals are not going to evangelize the world by themselves. The charismatics are not going to evangelize the world by themselves. God chose an evangelical and a charismatic to meet in the hallway and do the spiritual warfare. And to seal it, He chose Bill Bright, one of the Lausanne movement's most visible evangelical participants, to pray the healing prayer and watch God raise up Juana Francisco from her deathbed.

TERRITORIAL SPIRITS

Previous to Lausanne II in Manila there had not been much discussion about how territorial spirits could influence world evangelization even among Pentecostals and charismatics, to say nothing about evangelicals. Although the subject was not part of the overall design of the program committee, five of the workshops at Manila dealt with territorial spirits and strategic-level spiritual intercession. Those who addressed the issue were Omar Cabrera and Edgardo Silvoso of Argentina, Rita Cabezas of Costa Rica, and Tom White and I from the United States. The interest in these workshops exceeded expectations, and I sensed before we left that God wanted me to take some leadership in further research on the subject.

John Robb of World Vision precipitated the convening of a very select group of those living in the United States who had acquired some knowledge of strategic-level spiritual warfare. Almost by default, I became the coordinator of the event. Prominent among the 30 individuals who attended the first meeting in Pasadena, California, on February 12, 1990, were Larry Lea, Gary Clark, John Dawson, Cindy Jacobs, Dick Bernal, Edgardo Silvoso, Mary Lance Sisk, Gwen Shaw, Frank Hammond, Bobbie Jean Merck, Jack Hayford, Joy Dawson, Beth Alves, Ed Murphy, Tom White, Charles Kraft and many others. Bobbye Byerly led a simultaneous intercession group who prayed in the next room throughout the meeting.

The group began to call itself "The Spiritual Warfare Network" with the subtitle: "A Post-Lausanne II in Manila Group Studying Strategic-Level Spiritual Warfare." None of the members of the Spiritual Warfare Network considers himself or herself an expert, but all agree that the real battle for world evangelization is spiritual, and that the more we learn about it the more effectively we will be able to complete the Great Commission of Jesus to make disciples of all nations.

Some in the group are moving ahead on this. John Dawson's excellent book, *Taking Our Cities for God* (Creation House) is the first analytical and instructional book we have on warfare prayer. Dick Bernal's books such as *Storming Hell's Brazen Gates* (Jubilee Christian Center) and *Come Down Dark Prince* (Companion Press) share actual field ministries of warfare prayer. My book, *Engaging the Enemy* (Regal Books), brings together writings on the subject by 18 Christian leaders such as Tom White, Dick Bernal, Larry Lea, Jack Hayford, John Dawson, Edgardo Silvoso of the Spiritual Warfare Network, Michael Green, Paul Yonggi Cho, Timothy Warner, Oscar Cullmann and others. Cindy Jacobs' *Possessing the Gates of the Enemy* (Chosen Books) is the practical textbook on how we actually do the intercession. The important concept of "spiritual mapping" (see chapter 8) is introduced in George Otis, Jr.'s, *The Last of the Giants* (Chosen Books).

SPIRITUAL POWER IN EVANGELISM

Not everyone who sets out to evangelize is equally effective. Since that is the case, it is helpful to know who is the most effective and what things they may be doing that others aren't. This is one of the tasks of professors of church growth like me. I have been studying the growth and non-growth of churches for more than two decades and some of the answers have been emerging.

Church growth is somewhat complex. Three sets of factors enter the picture when analyzing growth or decline of churches. *Institutional factors,* the church can change if it wishes. *Contextual factors,* which are sociological conditions, the church has no power to change. Finally, *spiritual factors, which* reflect the hand of our sovereign God.

When looked at on a global scale, however, it seems that the institutional and contextual factors may not be as crucial as the spiritual factors. This becomes evident when one looks at the growth of the Pentecostal and charismatic movements in the past 40 or 50 years. Although some vigorous growth has occurred among non-charismatics and not all charismatic-type churches and denominations are growing, the fact remains that through recent decades the most amazing church growth worldwide has been seen among the churches that most explicitly depend on spiritual power, namely the Pentecostal and charismatic churches.

The Pentecostal/charismatic movement has its roots in the

In all of human history not another non-militaristic, non-political voluntary human movement has grown as dramatically as the Pentecostal/charismatic movement has grown over the past 25 years.

---

beginning of the twentieth century, but its vigorous growth did not really begin until after World War II. At that time, in 1945, it counted 16 million adherents worldwide. By 1965 it had grown to 50 million, by 1985 to 247 million, and the 1991 figure is an incredible 391 million.

One Pentecostal denomination, the Assemblies of God, grew from 1.6 million in 1965 to 13.2 million in 1985. Even though it is a relatively new denomination, the Assemblies of God is now the largest or second largest denomination in more than 30 nations of the world. In one city alone, São Paulo, Brazil, the Assemblies of God reports 2,400 churches. The fastest growing Christian movement in the United States is the independent charismatics. With some exceptions, the largest megachurch in almost any American metropolitan area is Pentecostal or charismatic. All 6 of the world's churches that had a 1990 worship attendance of 50,000 or more are Pentecostal/ charismatic.

Although I am not a professional historian, I would be bold enough to advance a hypothesis. *I would think that in all of human history not another non-militaristic, non-political voluntary human movement has grown as dramatically as the Pentecostal/charismatic movement has grown over the past 25 years.*

It seems reasonable to assume that those of us, like me, who come from the traditional evangelical wing of the church would do well to be open to learn from our charismatic brothers and sisters. The most fundamental lesson, as I see it, is that they have a more advanced understanding that the real battle for evangelization is spiritual. Signs and wonders, deliverance from demonic powers, miraculous healings, sustained and enthusiastic worship, prophecies and warfare prayer are seen by many of them as the normal outworking of Christianity.

The manifestation of this spiritual power in bringing large numbers of people to Jesus Christ speaks for itself. We need only observe what God is doing in the world today to realize that the effectiveness of our evangelistic efforts depends to a great degree on the outcome of the spiritual battles in the heavenly places.

The Scriptures indicate that our chief weapon for engaging the enemy in this battle is warfare prayer.

■ REFLECTION QUESTIONS ■

1. Discuss some evangelistic methodology or church growth techniques you know about that do not seem to be working as well as they might.
2. How would you describe each segment of the "threefold

cord" God is bringing together? Name some leaders of each. Can you see them supporting each other's ministry?

3. Do you believe that Christians like Juana Francisco can really be cursed? Could she have died if the curse had not been broken?

4. If you were to attend a meeting of the Spiritual Warfare Network, what topics would you like to hear discussed?

5. Name several of the specific areas the rest of the Body of Christ can learn from the Pentecostal/charismatic movement.

Jesus on the Offensive

CHAPTER THREE

I F JESUS' PUBLIC MINISTRY BEGAN WITH HIS BAPTISM, HIS first act of public ministry involved the highest degree of strategic-level spiritual warfare. "Jesus was led up by the Spirit into the wilderness to be tempted by the devil" (Matt. 4:1).

The Old Testament does not have a parallel account of this type of activity. Jesus introduced something new to the history of salvation. By engaging the enemy in the highest level power encounter, Jesus was serving notice to him and to the whole world that the battle was on. The Kingdom of God had come!

THE KINGDOM IS HERE

The message that the Kingdom of God had come was prominent in the preaching of John the Baptist, Jesus and the apostles. The reason we see the phrase "Repent, for the Kingdom of God is at hand" so much in the Gospels is that it signifies the most radical turning point in the history of humanity since the Fall of Adam and Eve. The turning point encompassed Jesus' incarnation, virgin birth, baptism, ministry, death and resurrection. The broader application throughout the rest of history began on the day of Pentecost.

Jesus' coming was such a radical event because previously Satan had enjoyed almost unlimited power here on Earth. This is not to ignore the fact that God is ultimately the King of kings, the Lord of lords and the Creator of the entire universe, including Satan. Satan is a mere creature who at one point never existed and who will ultimately find himself in a lake of fire, dearly wishing he had never been created in the first place (see Rev. 20:10). In the meantime, however, biblical descriptions of Satan must not be taken lightly. He is called "the god of this age" (2 Cor. 4:4), "the prince of the power of the air" (Eph. 2:2) and "the ruler of this world" (John 12:31). John affirms that "the whole world lies under the sway of the wicked one" (1 John 5:19). This is awesome language.

If we think Satan has formidable power these days, we must realize he had even more power before Jesus came. When Jesus came, He announced that He was introducing the Kingdom of God and engaged the enemy in a battle, which continues today. Satan knew full well that "the Son of God was manifested, that He might destroy the works of the devil" (1 John 3:8), and he was furious that his kingdom was being invaded. Jesus not only invaded Satan's kingdom, but He defeated him decisively on the cross as Paul so vividly describes in Colossians, saying that Jesus on the cross "disarmed principalities and powers" and "made a public spectacle of them, triumphing over them in it" (Col. 2:15).

Even before the cross, Jesus was able to say that till then no one in Old Testament times had been greater than John the

Baptist, "he who is least in the kingdom of heaven is greater than he" (Matt. 11:11). He could announce the ultimate victory some three years before it was actually accomplished on the cross, because the devil had already been defeated at the power encounter, which we commonly call Jesus' temptation.

JESUS PROVOKES THE CONFLICT

Instead of going about His business and allowing Satan to choose the time and place of attack, Jesus took the initiative and went on the offensive immediately after His baptism. Before He announced His agenda in the synagogue of Nazareth, before He called the 12 disciples, before He preached the Sermon on the Mount, before He fed 5,000 or raised Lazarus from the dead, He knew He must engage in some crucial strategic-level spiritual warfare.

The place Jesus chose is significant. He went to the "wilderness," which was known as a territory of Satan. The *Dictionary of New Testament Theology* says of *eremos,* the Greek word for wilderness or desert, that it is "a place of deadly danger...and of demonic powers" and "only where God's judgment has fallen is there victory over the desert and its maleficent spirits."[1] If Jesus' encounter with the devil was to be decisive, he should be given, to use an athletic term, "home field advantage." Jesus moved in on the devil's turf without hesitation and without fear.

Satan knew what the stakes were, and he gave it his best shot. He went so far as to offer Jesus his most priceless possession, "all the kingdoms of the world and their glory" (Matt. 4:8). It was a crucial and ferocious battle, but the outcome was never in doubt. Satan's power never has been nor ever will be a match for the power of God. Jesus won. Satan was defeated. The power encounter cleared the way spiritually for all that

Jesus was to accomplish over the next three years, including His death and resurrection.

CAN WE IDENTIFY WITH THIS?

Some at this point may be reasoning that Jesus was able to engage in such a power encounter because He is God, the second person of the Trinity. Since none of us is God, we therefore cannot identify with this kind of spiritual warfare.

This is such a crucial issue that I am going to get theological and discuss the relationship of the two natures of Christ. Let me say up front that I believe a key to understanding how our ministry today reflects or does not reflect the ministry of Jesus is understanding what systematic theologian Colin Brown calls "Spirit Christology"[2] and what I have referred to as "incarnation theology." I explain this in some detail in my book, *How to Have a Healing Ministry* (Regal), so I will only summarize it here.

My theological premise is the following: "The Holy Spirit was the source of all of Jesus' power during His earthly ministry. Jesus exercised no power of or by Himself. We today can expect to do the same or greater things than Jesus did because we have been given access to the same power source."[3]

While holding firm to the fact that at all times Jesus was totally God and totally human during His earthly ministry, it is clear from His own words, "the Son can do nothing of Himself, but what He sees the Father do" (John 5:19). According to Philippians 2, Jesus voluntarily became obedient to the Father during His incarnation on Earth (see Phil. 2:5-8). He agreed to forgo the use of His divine attributes for a season. He did no miraculous works by His divine nature, for if He had done so He would have violated His pact of obedience with the Father. All of His miraculous works were done by the Holy Spirit operating through Him. (See Matt. 12:28; Acts 10:38; Luke 4:1,14; 5:17.) Colin Brown therefore calls this "Spirit Christology."

This is why, when Jesus was ready to leave the Earth, He could truthfully tell His disciples it would be to their advantage for Him to go (see John 16:7). Only after He left could He send them the Holy Spirit to be their *Paraclete* (John 16:14). Jesus said, "Most assuredly, I say to you, he who believes in Me, the works that I do he will do also; and greater works than these will he do, because I go to My Father" (John 14:12).

THE MEANING OF JESUS' TEMPTATION

Back now to the power encounter at Jesus' temptation. I mentioned previously that Satan gave it his best shot, but what specifically was Satan's plan of attack?

Satan attacked Jesus precisely as he attacked Adam and Eve in the first temptation, at the point of obedience to God. Satan succeeded in enticing Adam and Eve to disobey God, and he expected he would succeed with Jesus as well. Knowing that if Jesus ever broke the pact of obedience He had made with the Father the plan of salvation would be over, Satan went for it three times. Jesus could have turned the stones into bread and He could have hurled Himself off the Temple and called angels to His rescue, but in either case He would have had to use His divine attributes, which He always had the power to do. He could have asserted His deity and taken the kingdoms from Satan *without* worshiping him. But since the Father had not instructed Him to do any of these three things, Jesus didn't. Unlike Adam and Eve, He obeyed the Father.

What we see, then, is Jesus in His *human* nature confronting the enemy directly. True, He was always the second person of the Trinity, but that was only incidental to the nature of this power encounter. The central fact was that Jesus, as a *human being,* openly challenged Satan on his territory and defeated him. This He did through the power of the Holy Spirit. During His baptism, the Holy Spirit came upon Him like a dove and He was filled with the Spirit (Mark 1:10). Then He was "led by the Spirit" to the power encounter with Satan (Luke 4:1). And after the devil was defeated, "Jesus returned in the power of the Spirit to Galilee" (Luke 4:14).

The question before us remains, can we today identify with this? Well, we can be tempted by the devil as Jesus was, since He was "in all points tempted as we are" (Heb. 4:15). And we have access to the same Holy Spirit (John 16:14). And furthermore Jesus said to His disciples, and presumably to us as well, "I give you the authority...over all the power of the enemy" (Luke 10:19). I myself believe we have the theological and spiritual potential to do the works that Jesus did.

But I hasten to point out this is largely a theoretical conclusion. Whether we *should* do this at all, and if so to what degree and under what circumstances, is a different and more immediate question.

HOW FAR SHOULD WE GO?

One of the reasons we need to exercise caution at this point is that we have no biblical examples of the 12 apostles or any other first-century Christian leaders who challenged the devil to a direct power encounter as Jesus did. I would surmise the best explanation for this may be that God did not direct them to do so. Apparently the Holy Spirit did not lead any of them to the literal wilderness or to an equivalent power encounter scenario as He did Jesus. If the disciples followed Jesus' example and did only what they saw the Father doing, we can conclude that the Father quite obviously was not doing this.

What happens when Christians today shout, "I bind you, Satan!"? Perhaps not as much as we would hope. Satan will eventually be bound for 1,000 years, but it will be an angel who does it, not a human being (see Rev. 20:1-2). On the other hand, saying "I bind you, Satan!" may serve the useful function of declaring to ourselves and to others in no uncertain terms that we do not like the devil at all, and that we want to see him neutralized to the degree possible.

I would not be among those who scold brothers and sisters who aggressively rebuke the devil any more than I would criticize an American soldier in the Persian Gulf who would shout, "Here we come, Saddam Hussein!" None of the soldiers even expected to see Saddam Hussein personally, but they did declare who the real enemy was.

Jesus helps us understand this. He cast a spirit of infirmity out of a woman who had been bound by the spirit for 18 years. Then later, when explaining what He had done, He said that *Satan* had kept her bound for 18 years (see Luke 13:10-16). I don't think Jesus meant that Satan *himself* had spent 18 years demonizing that woman, but that he had been ultimately responsible, as commander-in-chief of the forces of evil, of delegating that task to a certain spirit of infirmity. So while Jesus can say that Satan bound her, it is appropriate for us to say, "I bind you, Satan!" providing we understand the limitations of such an activity.

While therefore it may be doubtful God expects us to have a direct confrontation with Satan himself, at the same time there is little doubt that we do have a divine mandate to confront the demonic on levels lower than Satan. New Testament examples are so numerous they need not be rehearsed. Jesus clearly connected preaching the kingdom of heaven with casting out demons (see Matt. 10:7,8).

What Jesus did not specify, however, is whether our expected encounter with the demonic would be only on the ground level of spiritual warfare, which is quite obvious, or whether it would move upward to include occult-level or strategic-level warfare as well. On this point there remains some disagreement among those who actively teach on and engage in spiritual warfare these days. Our general agreement, so far as I can perceive it, is that we are to minister quite freely on the ground level casting out ordinary demons, and that we do well to stay away from direct encounters with the god of this age, Satan himself. Some are more cautious about engaging demonic forces at the in-between levels, while others are more aggressive.

I myself feel that God may be calling, equipping and enabling a relatively small number of Christian leaders to move out in frontline, strategic-level spiritual warfare. And I also believe He is raising up large numbers of Christians to back up these people with moral support, intercession, encouragement and material resources. God, I think, is in the process of choosing an expanding corps of spiritual Green Berets such as Eduardo Lorenzo, Cindy Jacobs, Larry Lea, Carlos Annacondia, John Dawson, Edgardo Silvoso or Dick Bernal who will engage in the crucial high-level battles against the rulers of darkness and consequently see measurable increases in the numbers of lost people who "turn them from darkness to light, and from the power of Satan to God" (Acts 26:18).

CONQUERING A CITY

What did Jesus have to say to His followers about strategic-level spiritual warfare? Some of His most direct instructions are found not in the Gospels, but rather in the book of Revelation. It is not unusual to forget that more than two full chapters in Revelation are the literal words of Jesus. My Bible reminds me because they are printed in red ink. The content of the letters to the seven churches in Asia is one of the few parts of the Bible that apparently were literally dictated by God to the human author.

The seven different churches receive seven different messages. Nevertheless, they have some things in common. For example, each letter begins with some descriptive phrases about the author, Jesus Christ. Each letter affirms that its contents are "what the Spirit says to the churches." And, most importantly for us here, only one command-type verb is used in each of the seven letters: *overcome*.

In fact, some rather extravagant promises are attached to overcoming in each of the letters. If we overcome, as Jesus desires us to, we will (1) eat from the tree of life, (2) not be hurt by the second death, (3) eat of the hidden manna, (4) have

---

Satan's central task and desire is to prevent God from being glorified.

---

power over the nations, (5) be clothed in white garments, (6) be a pillar in the temple in the New Jerusalem, and (7) sit with Jesus on His throne. Big-time rewards await those who comply!

But what does it mean to "overcome"? Since this seems to be such a crucial item on Jesus' agenda for the ongoing church, a word study is in order. The Greek word for overcome is *nikao*, the root of the common Greek name, Nicholas or Nick. It means "to conquer" and is a prominent warfare term. When Jesus calls us to overcome, He calls us to spiritual warfare. The *Dictionary of New Testament Theology* says that in the New Testament, nikao "almost always presupposes the conflict between God or Christ and opposing demonic powers."[4]

Other parts of the New Testament record Jesus using nikao on only two other occasions. One is in John 16:33 where Jesus affirms, "I have overcome [nikao] the world." This is a tremendously reassuring passage because it reminds us that the war itself is over and the winner and the loser have already been determined. It is not our job to win the war, Jesus did that on the cross. Ours is the mop-up operation. But Jesus still expects us to overcome.

OVERCOMING THE STRONGMAN

The other time Jesus uses nikao is in one of His references to dealing with the "strongman," or with an opposing demonic force. In Luke's Gospel, He speaks of overcoming (nikao) the strongman so that his palace can be invaded and his goods spoiled. This not only is a significant spiritual warfare passage, but it could reasonably be taken to apply to multi-leveled demonic activity. The incident begins with ground-level spiritual warfare as Jesus casts a demon out of a mute (Luke 11:14). But Jesus then goes on to talk about Satan's kingdom (Luke 11:18) and a palace (Luke 11:21) and Beelzebub who is a high prince of demons but ranked under Satan himself. This could be seen as an escalation of Jesus' scope of conquering or overcoming.

In the parallel passages on the strongman in Matthew and Mark, Jesus does not use the word for "overcome," but the word for "bind" (see Matt. 12:29 and Mark 3:27). It is the same word used in Matthew 16:19 where Jesus says, "Whatever you bind on earth will be bound in heaven." We are justified, therefore, to use interchangeably the terms "overcome," "conquer" or "bind" when we describe our activity in taking the offensive against the enemy in spiritual warfare.

The churches in the seven cities are to overcome or conquer the forces of evil preventing the glory of God from shining in their cities. I take that as Jesus' desire, not only for the first century, but for us in the twentieth century as well. For example, I feel a responsibility for conquering my city of Pasadena, California, for Christ. I have the privilege of participating in a larger group of Christian leaders called "Pasadena for Christ." At this point we are only in the beginning stages of launching a massive effort at warfare prayer for our city. We sincerely hope that eventually we will be able to identify the strongman or strongmen over Pasadena and to overcome in obedience to Jesus' directive.

SATAN'S STRATEGY

Overcoming the strategic-level demonic forces ruling a city demands a basic understanding of Satan's modus operandi.

I think it is accurate to summarize all the evil and tactical activities of Satan in this statement: *Satan's central task and desire is to prevent God from being glorified.* Whenever God is not glorified in a person's life, in a church, in a city or in the world as a whole, Satan has to that degree accomplished his objective. The underlying motivation, as we are fully aware, is that Satan himself wants the glory due to God. As Lucifer fell from heaven, he was exclaiming, "I will be like the Most High!" (Isa. 14:14). He tempted Adam and Eve by telling them that if they ate the forbidden fruit "you will be like God" (Gen. 3:5). He unsuccessfully tried to tempt Jesus into worshiping and glorifying him (Matt. 4:9).

How does Satan go about keeping God from being glorified? To answer this question, it seems helpful to separate his activities into primary objectives and secondary objectives.

Satan's primary objective is to prevent God from being glorified by keeping lost people from being saved. Jesus came to seek and to save the lost. God sent His Son that whosoever believes on Him should have everlasting life. Whenever a person is saved, the angels in heaven rejoice. Satan hates all of the above. He wants people to go to hell, not to heaven. And the reason this is his primary objective is that each time he succeeds he has won an *eternal victory.*

Satan's secondary objective is to make human beings and human society as miserable as possible in this present life. The enemy has come to steal, to kill and to destroy. When we see wars, poverty, oppression, sickness, racism, greed and similar evils too numerous to list, we have no doubt that Satan is succeeding all too much. None of these things brings glory to God. But these are secondary objectives because each is only a *temporal victory*.

Satan is skilled at both tactics. He has accumulated millennia of experience. I agree with Timothy Warner who says, "Satan's chief tactic is deception" and he does it "by telling people lies about God" and "by deceiving them through his shows of power."[5] How he so massively prevents people from believing the gospel is almost incomprehensible to me.

Why is it that when we share the gospel with our neighbors they don't even hear what we are saying much of the time? The gospel is such a good deal. The benefits are enormous. Becoming a Christian is better than winning the lottery! Yet many of our neighbors would prefer the lottery to eternal life. Why? The answer is clear in 2 Corinthians 4:3,4. The apostle Paul was experiencing similar frustration. Not enough people were accepting Christ. So he said the gospel is veiled to those who are perishing "whose minds the god of this age has blinded,...lest the light of the gospel of the glory of Christ,...should shine on them" (2 Cor. 4:4). People do not become Christians pure and simple because their minds are blinded. The glory of Christ does not penetrate to them. Satan is doing his thing!

BLINDING THREE BILLION MINDS

As I write, 3 billion individuals on Planet Earth do not yet know Jesus Christ as Lord and Savior. And this doesn't even count millions of others who are Christian in name only but not in heart commitment. My point is that Satan is getting away with a lot. But how does he do it? How does he blind 3 billion or more minds?

Obviously, Satan cannot do it by himself. Satan is not God, nor does he possess any of the attributes of God. This means among other things that Satan is not omnipresent. He cannot be in all places at all times as God is. Satan can be in only one place at one time. He may be able to get from one place to another very rapidly, but when he is there, he is still in only one place.

The only way I can imagine that Satan can effectively blind 3 billion minds is to delegate the responsibility. He maintains a hierarchy of demonic forces to carry out his purposes. Exactly what that hierarchy is we may never know, but we do have some general indications. Perhaps our clearest hint is found in Ephesians 6:12 where we are told that we wrestle not against flesh and blood, but against (1) principalities, (2) powers, (3) rulers of the darkness of this age, and (4) spiritual hosts of wickedness in the heavenly places.

New Testament scholars cannot find a strict hierarchical order in Ephesians 6:12 since the same Greek terms are used with different meanings and interchangeably in other parts of Scripture. And other terms such as "thrones" and "dominions" are added elsewhere. In other words, these categories are not as clear as generals, colonels, majors and captains would be to us. What is clear, however, is that the terms do describe certain varieties of supernatural, demonic beings whose assignment is to implement "the wiles of the devil" (Eph. 6:11). These beings, and perhaps many other kinds who are under them and obey their instructions, are in charge of keeping lost people from being saved and for messing up their lives as much as possible while they are on earth.

SEEING OUR CITIES AS THEY REALLY ARE

As I have mentioned, George Otis, Jr., is working on a fascinating concept, which he calls "spiritual mapping." Among other things, he says we need to strive to see our cities and our nations as they *really are*, not as they *appear to be*. It is crucial to discern the spiritual forces in the heavenlies that are shaping our visible lives here on earth. Walter Wink, for example, has been trying to convince social activists that bigger and better reform programs have not nor in all probability ever will change society for the better if the spiritual powers behind social structures are not named, unmasked and engaged.[6]

Frank Peretti, in his best-selling novels, *This Present Darkness* and *Piercing the Darkness* (Crossway Books), personalizes and dramatizes the struggle with the powers more than Walter Wink might be inclined. Although their approaches differ from each other and mine differs from both, the point is that we are striving to see our world as it really is, not simply as it appears to be.

One of the most helpful biblical passages is 2 Corinthians 10:3 where Paul says, "For though we walk in the flesh, we do not war according to the flesh." Jesus said we are supposed to be in this world, but not of this world (see John 15:19 and John 17:15). This means the real battle is a spiritual battle. In 2 Corinthians, Paul goes on to say:

> For the weapons of our warfare are not carnal but mighty in God for pulling down strongholds, casting down arguments and every high thing that exalts itself against the knowledge of God, bringing every thought into captivity to the obedience of Christ (2 Cor. 10:4,5).

The stronghold is the place where the devil and his forces are entrenched. Pulling down strongholds is obviously an offensive warfare action. God apparently wants us to attack these strongholds much as Jesus invaded Satan's turf in the wilderness for His definitive power encounter. Charles Kraft makes a helpful distinction between three kinds of spiritual encounters. All are found in 2 Corinthians 10:4,5: truth encounter, allegiance encounter and power encounter.[7] The truth encounter is "casting down arguments" and the allegiance encounter is "bringing every thought into captivity to the obedience of Christ." Warfare prayer needs to be directed against these two kinds of strongholds.

The phrase that most directly addresses the demonic in 2 Corinthians 10:4,5 is, "every high thing that exalts itself against the knowledge of God." The Greek word for "high thing" is *hypsoma*, which according to the *Dictionary of New Testament Theology* is a term relating to "astrological ideas," "cosmic powers," and "powers directed against God, seeking to intervene between God and man."[8] This points to the need for engaging in strategic-level spiritual warfare, which will push back these powers or territorial spirits that keep God from being glorified.

If we see these powers we will see our cities as they really are. The crime, gangs, poverty, abortion, racism, greed, rape, drugs, divorce, social injustice, child abuse and other evils that characterize my city of Pasadena, California, reflect Satan's temporal victories. The empty churches and indifference to the gospel reflect Satan's eternal victories. I affirm and participate in promoting social programs, education, pro-life demonstrations, strong police forces and sound legislation. I believe in evangelistic crusades and the Four Spiritual Laws. But these social and evangelistic programs will never work as well as they could or should by themselves if Satan's strongholds are not torn down. This is the real battle, and our weapon is prayer. Warfare prayer.

BIBLICAL EXAMPLES

Once we come to understand the biblical and theological principles behind Jesus' wilderness encounter with the enemy, His desire that we "overcome" or conquer our cities for Christ, and the nature of the real battle, which is a spiritual one, several other biblical passages take on a new meaning. I see them not so much as tactical manuals for Christians who are called to strategic-level spiritual warfare as simply illustrations of how God used His servants from time to time in warfare prayer.

Daniel

A common example is the experience of Daniel the prophet who engaged in three weeks of warfare prayer along with fasting (Dan. 10:1-21). He was praying over issues that were directed to the highest political realm involving Cyrus, king of Persia. Daniel was praying for concerns in the natural, sociopolitical realm, but in this case we are given a rare glimpse of what actually happened in the spiritual realm as a result of Daniel's prayer. We are shown the kingdom of Persia as it really is, not only as it appears to be.

During his season of prayer and fasting, Daniel had a "great vision," which left him with "no strength" (Dan. 10:8). But then an angel appeared to Daniel in person to tell him what had happened. This angel had been dispatched to go to Daniel on the first day of his praying, but it took him 21 days to arrive. The three-week interval saw a fierce spiritual battle in the heavenlies. The demonic being named the "Prince of Persia" was able to block the progress of this good angel until reinforcements arrived in the person of none less than Michael the archangel. He gave Daniel a message from God, which was so awesome that Daniel "turned [his] face toward the ground and became speechless" (Dan. 10:15). Then the angel told Daniel that on his return trip he not only would have to battle the Prince of Persia but also the Prince of Greece and that again he would only get through with Michael's help.

This story leaves us little doubt that territorial spirits greatly influence human life in all its sociopolitical aspects. And it also shows us clearly that the only weapon Daniel had to combat these rulers of darkness was warfare prayer.

Jeremiah

We do not have the same detail of the war in the heavenlies accompanying the ministry of Jeremiah the prophet, but we have even greater detail of his divine call to strategic-level spiritual warfare. God said to Jeremiah, "See, I have this day set you over the nations and over the kingdoms, to root out and to pull down, to destroy and to throw down, to build and to plant" (Jer. 1:10). This, obviously, is not a reference to the kingdoms of this world as they appear to be, but as they really are. It is a reference to the principalities and powers, which are at the root of what takes place in human affairs.

And God did not give Jeremiah carnal weapons to do this work. He had no political office or military command or vast wealth at his disposal. His weapon was intercession, warfare prayer that was in tune with God and powerful enough to change the course of human history.

Luke and Acts

Few modern scholars have so painstakingly looked into the theme of strategic-level spiritual warfare in the New Testament as has the Yale New Testament scholar, Susan R. Garrett. Her excellent book, *The Demise of the Devil,* confirms that the underlying theme of Luke's narrative in the book of Acts was the battle against the demonic. Susan Garrett raises the question: "If people's eyes have been 'blinded' by Satan's control over their lives, how can Paul open them?" The answer, she affirms, is: *"Paul must himself be invested with authority that is greater than Satan's own"* (emphasis hers). She sees a key passage in Luke as being Jesus' declaration that His disciples would have authority over all the power of the enemy (Luke 10:19) and this is exactly the power that operates through Paul in Acts.[9]

It might well be that the most outstanding example we have of the apostle Paul "taking the city for God," to use John Dawson's terminology, is his ministry in the city of Ephesus. Ephesus stood among cities in the Roman empire as a "center for magical powers" according to Talbot School of Theology professor Clinton E. Arnold. Arnold affirms that "the overriding characteristic of the practice of magic throughout the Hellenistic world was the cognizance of a spirit world exercising influence over virtually every aspect of life."[10] When Paul went

---

Through the ministry of the apostle Paul and others on his team, the principalities over the area [Ephesus] were weakened to the extent that the gospel could then spread rapidly. This was effective strategic-level spiritual warfare.

---

to Ephesus, he must have known something of the intense high-level spiritual warfare that awaited him. And after he left, his epistle to the Ephesians contained "a substantially higher concentration of power terminology than in any other epistle attributed to Paul."[11]

Paul's ministry in Ephesus resulted in planting a strong church there as well as establishing a regional base for extensive evangelistic outreach. During two years "all who dwelt in Asia heard the word of the Lord Jesus" (Acts 19:10), and "the word of the Lord grew mightily and prevailed" (Acts 19:20). Susan Garrett says the phrase "growth of the word" signifies that an obstacle had been overcome. What was the obstacle? She says, "It was the seemingly relentless grip that the practice of magic—the trafficking in evil spirits and concomitant loyalty to their master, the devil—had exercised on the Ephesian people."[12] In other words, through the ministry of the apostle

Paul and others on his team, the principalities over the area were weakened to the extent that the gospel could then spread rapidly. This was effective strategic-level spiritual warfare, interpreted by many as an assault on the known territorial spirit, Diana of the Ephesians.

Previous to his experience in Ephesus, Paul experienced another high-level power encounter in western Cyprus where he discovered that the political leader, Sergius Paulus, had linked up with an occult practitioner, Elymas or Bar-Jesus. The sorcerer did what Satan desired, seeking "to turn the proconsul away from the faith." After making certain the general public recognized that this man was "full of all deceit and all fraud" and a "son of the devil" and an "enemy of righteousness," Paul, by the power of the Holy Spirit, struck him blind. Susan Garrett comments, "When Paul invoked the hand of the Lord, causing mist and darkness to fall upon Bar-Jesus, Paul's possession of greater authority than Satan is unmistakably confirmed." The people there quickly perceived that "Truly this man is one able to open the eyes of the Gentiles, that they might turn from darkness to light and from the authority of Satan to God."[13]

Bible-believing Christians will want to follow Jesus and the apostles in the strategic-level spiritual warfare that can lead to conquering their cities and nations for Christ. I like the way Susan Garrett describes the world surrounding the ministry of Jesus and the apostles: "The dark regions are the realm of Satan, the ruler of this world, who for eons has sat entrenched and well-guarded, his many possessions gathered like trophies around him. The sick and possessed are held captive by his demons; the Gentiles, too, are subject to his dominion, giving him honor and glory that ought to be offered to God."[14]

When Jesus came announcing the Kingdom of God, this dark kingdom of Satan was doomed. Garrett says, "To be sure, the final victory lay in the future. But no longer could Satan and his demonic and human servants harass and torment at will. Satan's kingdom was splintering around him, and his authority was no longer acknowledged by all. The battle still raged but Christ's ultimate triumph was certain. Christian experience—from the earliest days to Luke's present—testified to the demise of the devil."[15]

■ REFLECTION QUESTIONS ■

1. Discuss the concept that Jesus lived His life on earth through His human nature, but at the same time He was always God.
2. What are the strengths and also the limitations of declaring, "I bind you, Satan"?
3. Explain how Satan goes about his task of preventing God from being glorified.
4. Looking at your own city "as it really is" and not just "as it appears to be," what would you likely find?
5. What was involved in the apostle Paul's spiritual warfare against Diana of the Ephesians?

Notes
1. O. Bocher, "Wilderness," *The New International Dictionary of New Testament Theology,* Colin Brown, ed., Vol. 3, pp. 1005, 1008 (Grand Rapids, MI: Zondervan Publishing House, 1978).
2. Colin Brown, *That You May Believe: Miracles and Faith Then and Now* (Grand Rapids, MI: Wm. B. Eerdmans Pub. Co., 1985).
3. C. Peter Wagner, *How to Have a Healing Ministry* (Ventura, CA: Regal Books, 1989), p. 114.
4. W. Gunther, "Fight," *Dictionary of New Testament Theology,* Vol. 1, p. 650.
5. Timothy M. Warner, "Deception: Satan's Chief Tactic," *Wrestling with Dark Angels,* C. Peter Wagner and F. Douglas Pennoyer, eds. (Ventura, CA: Regal Books, 1990), pp. 102-103.
6. Walter Wink's influential trilogy includes *Naming the Powers, Unmasking the Powers,* and *Engaging the Powers,* all published by Fortress Press.
7. Charles H. Kraft, "Encounter in Christian Witness," *Evangelical Missions Quarterly,* July 1991, pp. 258-265.
8. D. Mueller, "Height," *Dictionary of New Testament Theology,* Vol. 2, p. 200.

9. Susan R. Garrett, *The Demise of the Devil: Magic and the Demonic in Luke's Writings* (Minneapolis, MN: Fortress Press, 1989), p. 84.
10. Clinton E. Arnold, *Ephesians: Power and Magic* (Cambridge, England: Cambridge University Press, 1989), pp. 14, 18.
11. Ibid., p. 1.
12. Garrett, *The Demise of the Devil*, p. 97.
13. Ibid., p. 86.
14. Ibid., p. 101.
15. Ibid., pp. 108-109.

Demons Behind Bushes

CHAPTER FOUR

RICHARD COLLINGRIDGE HAS BEEN A FOREIGN MISSIONARY for more than 20 years. I first met him in the late 1980s when he was taking time out to do graduate studies in missiology in our Fuller Seminary School of World Mission. He is a mature, spiritual and emotionally-balanced person. I say that because I suspect ahead of time that some who read the story he tells would otherwise desire to relegate him to what they consider the "lunatic fringe."

THE "WATER DEVIL"

Back in 1975, Rich had been teaching in the Sinoe Bible Institute in Liberia for five years. Some of his students had been telling him of a "water devil," which took the form of a brass ring and was often seen rolling down jungle trails under its own power. He later did some research and found that this "water spirit" was also described in *Tribes of the Liberian Hinterland* by George Schwab.[1] It was common knowledge that its power could be neutralized by striking the ring with a machete, putting blood on it or throwing a banana leaf in its path.

Rich, in those days, thought such things were mere "superstition." They must have been figments of some collective tribal imagination that certainly could bear no resemblance to real-

---

Paul...explains to the Corinthians that before we even begin to talk about demons and idols we must remind ourselves that God is supreme over all created beings including demons and evil spirits.

---

ity in our scientific age. Out of a kind of anthropological curiosity, Collingridge asked his students if they could find one of these rolling demons for him to add to his collection of native art. A student soon located one, and Rich purchased it from a nearby villager. He decided to use the water devil as a doorstop in the family's front room.

Bad move!

Trouble began to pour in on the Collingridge family.

Rich's wife, Esther, began suffering severe headaches. At first she attributed them to the stress of mothering, home schooling children, Bible school teaching and other pressures that most missionary wives experience. But these headaches were different. They were emotionally disturbing. They did not go away. And the pain they caused was not the usual headache pain. The pains were sharper and more driving, and they came in strange parts of the head.

Their two young daughters began to have terrible night-mares. They would hear and actually see mysterious things on the walls. They often could sleep only if Rich or Esther would light a candle and sleep in the room with them.

As time went on and the unnatural disturbances grew more severe, the family prayed against the forces of darkness. Then early one morning their prayers were answered. Rich sudden-ly came wide awake with the full knowledge of what was hap-pening in their home. God had revealed to him that they were under direct satanic attack through the water devil they had naively brought into their home. Rich shared with his wife what he had heard from the Lord, got out of bed, took the brass ring to the workshop, destroyed it with a sledge hammer, and threw it away.

A dramatic transformation immediately came over the Collingridge home. The attack was over and the victory was the Lord's. When Rich shared the experience with a mature, wise Liberian pastor, James Doe, the pastor simply nodded his head as if to say, "Well, what did you expect?"[2]

CAMPUS CRUSADE IN THAILAND

To my knowledge, the Campus Crusade for Christ *Jesus* film is the most powerful evangelistic tool operating in the world today. There can be little doubt that more people come to Christ through seeing the *Jesus* film than through any other sin-gle evangelistic resource. Paul Eshleman, the Campus Crusade executive in charge of the project, tells a fascinating story in his book, *I Just Saw Jesus*.

One of the outstanding examples of the fruit that can come through the *Jesus* film is the nation of Thailand. Up to the time that Campus Crusade began using the *Jesus* film in the early 1980s, only 500 churches had been established in Thailand dur-ing 150 years of missionary work. Since then, as Roy Rosedale's research has revealed, more than 2,000 new churches were planted in 8 years.[3]

Eshleman tells the story of the film team who had shown the film in a certain rural village. They had planned on staying in the village that night and returning home the next day. They were told they would be sleeping in the local Buddhist temple. What they were not told was that this particular temple was known for miles around as a chief dwelling place of demons. Others who had tried to sleep there had been run out before morning. Some reportedly had been found dead the next day.

Shortly after the team had gone to sleep, Eshleman reports, "they were awakened all at once by the immaterial presence of a hideous beast. There in the corner of the room appeared the most frightful image they had ever seen. Fear struck them all like an icy fist."[4]

The startled team decided to put into practice what they had seen Jesus do in their own film. They prayed together and boldly cast the demon out of the temple in the name of Jesus. Nothing else was necessary, and they slept peacefully the rest of the night.

In the early morning, the villagers came to carry off the team's equipment they were sure had been left behind when the Christians were run off or killed by the demons. When they found them sound asleep "they were confronted with the undeniable fact that God is more powerful than any other force."[5]

THE UNDERLYING ISSUE

A hypothesis I am attempting to defend in this book has been stated as follows:

> Satan delegates high ranking members of the hierarchy of evil spirits to control nations, regions, cities, tribes, people groups, neighborhoods and other significant

social networks of human beings throughout the world. Their major assignment is to prevent God from being glorified in their territory, which they do through directing the activity of lower ranking demons.[6]

It can immediately be seen that this hypothesis will stand or fall on the issue of whether spirits or demonic beings can legitimately be perceived as occupying territories. I will discuss that in detail in the next chapter, but first a preliminary question needs to be addressed: *Do demons attach themselves to specific things such as idols, animals, houses or natural features such as trees or mountains?*

My answer? Yes!

Matthew, Mark and Luke all tell the story of Jesus casting out the demon named Legion in the country of the Gadarenes. The demons went from the man into pigs (Matt. 8:28-34; Mark 5:1-20; Luke 8:26-39). There is no biblical question, then, that demons can attach themselves to animals.

Parenthetically, it is apropos to point out here that when they realized Jesus was going to cast them out of the man, the demons "begged Him earnestly that He would not send them out of the country" (Mark 5:10). Why did they do this? Obviously, remaining in the same geographical territory had some value to the demons, and Jesus acceded to their request, sending them into the pigs. Argentine pastor Eduardo Lorenzo, whose congregation was successful in evicting the territorial spirit over Adrogué (see chapter 1), reports their perception that principalities who are cast out of assigned territories fear cruel punishment will be inflicted by their spiritual superiors for their failure to remain. In Revelation 2:13, Satan is associated with a city and its cult-center. In the passage, the city of Pergamos in Asia Minor is said to be "where Satan dwells."

DEMONS AND IDOLS

A central biblical passage for understanding the relationship of
demons to idols is 1 Corinthians 8—10, where Paul deals with
the issue of eating meat offered to idols. He begins that extensive teaching by asserting that "we know that an idol is nothing
in the world, and that there is no other God but one" (1 Cor.
8:4). He later asks the rhetorical question: "What am I saying
then? That an idol is anything, or what is offered to idols is
anything?" (1 Cor. 10:19). The answer is, of course not. Paul
would agree with Isaiah who ridicules idol makers by saying,
"Who would form a god or cast a graven image that profits
him nothing?" (Isa. 44:10), and tells of a fool who uses half a
log to roast meat and the other half to make into a carved
image, then "he falls down before it and worships it, prays to
it and says, 'Deliver me, for you are my god'" (Isa. 44:17).

Paul also explains to the Corinthians that before we even
begin to talk about demons and idols we must remind ourselves that God is supreme over all created beings including
demons and evil spirits. Twice he cites Psalm 24:1: "The earth
is the Lord's, and all its fullness" (1 Cor. 10:26, 28). He is not
about to fall into a dualism in which forces of good and forces
of evil are seen to be on equal footing. No, Satan and all the
demons exercise only the power that God permits and no
more, as the book of Job clearly illustrates.

Having said this, we nevertheless put ourselves in dangerous and vulnerable positions if we do not see that objects such
as physical idols have the potential to harbor incredibly malignant power. This is, I believe, what is behind the first two of
the Ten Commandments: "You shall have no other gods before
Me" and "You shall not make for yourself any carved image"
(Exod. 20:3,4). Idols are not fun, games and playthings. *Dun-
geons and Dragons* is a qualitatively different game from *Scrab-
ble* or checkers. Frequently there is a pernicious relationship

between demonic beings and physical objects, even though the objects *in themselves* are only wood or metal or stone or plastic or whatever.

This is what Paul is attempting to explain to the Corinthians, some of whom were actually accepting invitations to enter idol temples and eating the meat that had been sacrificed there. Not that there was something intrinsically wrong with eating the meat itself. Knowing ahead of time that much of the meat sold in the public market had previously been sacrificed to idols, Paul nevertheless tells them to go ahead and eat it without asking any questions (see 1 Cor. 10:25). But the meat is one thing; the idol to whom it is sacrificed is something else.

Paul says the pagans are not simply sacrificing to a piece of wood or stone, but in the idol temple "the things which the Gentiles sacrifice they sacrifice to demons and not to God" (1 Cor. 10:20). New Testament scholar George Ladd, in commenting on this key passage, says there is "a power connected with idols that resides in demons. To worship idols therefore means to sacrifice to demons."[7] Leon Morris concurs: "When people sacrifice to idols, it cannot be said that they are engaging in some neutral activity that has no meaning. They are in fact sacrificing to evil spirits."[8]

This throws some biblical and scholarly light on incidences such as a water devil rolling down a Liberian jungle path or a Buddhist temple where resident demons are known to kill outsiders. Real demons do attach themselves to animals, idols, brass rings, trees, mountains, and buildings as well as to any number and variety of manufactured and natural objects.

DOES THIS HAPPEN IN THE UNITED STATES?

Many of my missionary friends from all parts of the world mention how risky it has been to relate their experiences with the demonic when they speak to congregations in the United

States, particularly in certain American church circles. One of the denominations that traditionally has been rather reluctant to accept challenges to vigorous spiritual warfare has been the Southern Baptists. I mention the Southern Baptists not to single them out for criticism but to congratulate them for hearing what the Spirit is saying to the churches. The February-March 1991 issue of *The Commission*, official publication of the Southern

---

We...put ourselves in dangerous and vulnerable positions if we do not see that objects such as physical idols have the potential to harbor incredibly malignant power.

Baptist Foreign Mission Board, carries remarkably frank articles on demonization and spiritual warfare.

After describing two rather startling demonic deliverances, one in the Caribbean and one in Malaysia, Leland Webb says, "Missionaries seldom share accounts like these with Baptists at home. One reason is that these reports fall outside the experience of most Christians in America."[9] He goes on to point out the obvious dilemma faced by those who hear such stories: If it happens on the mission field, why couldn't it happen here at home?

The fact of the matter, of course, is that it does happen here at home.

Like Southern Baptists, contemporary Mennonites have not been especially outspoken about demons and demonic manifestations. That in itself enhances the credibility of David W. Shenk and Ervin R. Stutzman, both Mennonites, who tell the story of a church-planting couple in New Jersey, Richard and Lois Landis. One of their church families became greatly troubled when their adolescent son kept waking up in the night by hearing mysterious scratching on his bedroom wall. Pastor Landis visited his room and found it cluttered with lewd rock 'n' roll pictures, objects and literature. The family repented, confessed, and cleaned out the room. "Then in the name of Jesus, they commanded the evil spirit who scratched the walls at night to leave forever." As a result of this simple act of faith accompanied with warfare prayer, "Peace filled the room and the Holy Spirit came upon that little group gathered with the lad in his bedroom. The evil spirit has never returned."[10]

SPIRITS IN THE WAGNER HOUSE

Not only can we bring the idea of spirits occupying houses back from the mission field to the United States, but I can also tell of spirits in my own home in Altadena, California.

Back in 1983 my wife, Doris, and I hosted an intercessory prayer group in our home once a month. One night two of the women who have gifts of discernment of spirits mentioned that they sensed a special presence of evil seemed to be located in the master bedroom. Not too long after that, one night when I was away, Doris woke up suddenly in the middle of the night with a powerful fear gripping her whole being. Her heart pounding furiously, she looked across the room and saw a shadowy form, about nine feet tall, with luminous green eyes and teeth. Her fear turned into anger, and she rebuked the spirit in the name of Jesus, commanding it to get out of her room and not to enter the children's rooms.

It left.

Some weeks later we were both in the bed when Doris awoke, this time with a piercing cramp in her foot. I laid hands on, prayed for healing, and tried to go back to sleep. In about ten minutes I asked how her foot was. She said, "The pain will not go, and I think it is a spirit." This time I rebuked the spirit in the name of Jesus. It apparently obeyed since the pain was immediately relieved and did not come back.

Two friends from our Sunday School class in Lake Avenue Congregational Church, Cathy Schaller and George Eckart, prayed fervently for Doris and me and were led of the Spirit to go into our house for warfare prayer. We gave them a house key one afternoon while we were working at the seminary. When they got out of their car they knew they were in for a battle since some invisible force physically prevented them from entering the patio surrounding the front door! They decided to go into the garage where they discerned several evil spirits, one so strong that Cathy could actually smell it. After casting them out, they could easily enter the patio and go into the house. They found spirits in three of the rooms, the strongest, predictably, in the master bedroom. In the living room they sensed that a spirit had attached itself to a stone puma we had brought as a souvenir from our missionary work in Bolivia.

When we got home we destroyed the puma as well as some animistic ceremonial masks we foolishly had mounted on our living room wall. The next time the intercession group met, they felt the atmosphere had changed and the house had been cleansed.

Wagner's Green-Eyed Monster

Our spirit incident was such an important learning experience for me that I wrote it up in a column in *Christian Life* magazine. When I did, I had no idea some students would post it on the Fuller Seminary "Board of Declaration" and make it the centerpiece for a vigorous campus debate, which lasted for about two weeks. Wagner's "green-eyed monster" became a laughing matter and a source of ridicule for many, while others defended it mainly by recounting similar experiences. One of the upshots was that I was called into the seminary president's office to give an account of my rather controversial behavior.

Although this experience was painful, much of the pain was relieved a few weeks later when I received a letter from Irene Warkentin of Winnipeg, Manitoba. She introduced herself as a teacher and sociologist with good academic credentials. And she told me how much my *Christian Life* column had meant to her when she read it. She said her five-year-old son, Kevin, had been experiencing severe leg cramps that had no medical explanation. She identified his cramps with Doris's cramps described in my article. So she went into Kevin's bedroom with a prayer that God would show her what was wrong. She says, "There it was—a dog statue brought from a foreign country." She sensed a clear word from the Holy Spirit that she was to destroy the statue.

After praying what I am calling a warfare prayer, Irene took the dog statue to the garage and smashed it with a hammer. She says, "I had done most everything in awe, but when I smashed that dog, the emotion I experienced was anger. I was so angry that I hit the dog with vehemence!" This, I might say, had special significance since Irene Warkentin is a Mennonite and by nature a very peaceful woman. Then, she says, the anger totally left. And, of course, the cramps in Kevin's legs ended once for all.

Second Opinions

I became so insecure because of the ridicule I received when I wrote the *Christian Life* column, I began to wonder whether I had gone off the deep end. So I searched the literature to see if others agreed. I was relieved to find many others who asserted with confidence that demons could, and indeed did, occupy certain houses and objects.

I was encouraged to find that British Anglican leader, Michael Harper, had a similar experience to mine. He, quite unexpectedly, began to be plagued with nighttime feelings of gloom and fear, especially the fear of death. This was so unusual for him that he became concerned, particularly when they steadily grew worse. He soon became convinced that the house his family had recently occupied, quite an old building, had "something unpleasant" about it. So he called on Dom Robert Petipierre, an Anglican Benedictine monk, to stay there for a night and do some warfare praying. Petipierre "conducted a Communion service in the house and exorcized every room" according to the prescribed Anglican ritual for such things. Michael Harper reports, "From that day onwards the atmosphere in the house changed and there was no recurrence of the experiences which I have related."[11]

The same Dom Robert Petipierre edited the report of a special commission to investigate such issues convened by the Bishop of Exeter in 1972. The Bishop described the situation that provoked him to form the commission as an attitude in the Church of England to "regard exorcism as an exercise in white magic or a survival of medieval superstition." It usually had been seen as a negative action. He was concerned that Anglican leaders had all but overlooked exorcism's "positive aspect as an extension of the frontiers of Christ's Kingdom and a demonstration of the power of the Resurrection to overcome evil and replace it with good."[12]

The report found that places such as churches, houses, towns and countryside may be strained and influenced by a variety of causes such as ghosts, magical spells, human sin, place memories, poltergeist or psychic action, and demonic influence.[13]

Respected Christian leaders such as missionary Vivienne Stacey tell about driving demons from haunted houses in Pakistan.[14] Pastor James Marocco describes the spiritual oppression on the Hawaiian island of Molokai.[15] Don Crawford reports spirits occupying a tree in Indonesia.[16] And the list could be extended ad infinitum.

DEMONS BEHIND BUSHES?

I fully realize that many feel uncomfortable with the notion that demons can and do attach themselves to material objects or houses or territories. A common expression used somewhat defensively is that people like Wagner or Petipierre or Collingridge or Irene Warkentin "see a demon behind every bush."

I must say that of the scores of Christian leaders I am in contact with who are involved in responsible deliverance ministries, I have not yet found one who would claim that a demon is behind every bush. But we do agree that demons are, in fact, behind some bushes. And to the degree that we are able by the power of the Holy Spirit to discern which bushes they are and the specific nature of the demonic infestations, the better able we are to take authority over them in Jesus' name and to reclaim territory they have usurped for the Kingdom of God.

In this book I want to attempt to use this discernment. I want to take seriously the admonition of C. S. Lewis in *The Screwtape Letters*: "There are two equal and opposite errors into which our race can fall about the devils. One is to disbelieve in their existence. The other is to believe, and to feel an excessive and unhealthy interest in them. They themselves are equally pleased by both errors, and hail a materialist and a magician with the same delight."[17]

▬ REFLECTION QUESTIONS ▬

1. What do you think of the story of Rick Collingridge's experience with the "water devil"? Have you ever seen or heard of anything like this?
2. Many people believe that houses can be haunted. Can evil spirits also dominate whole territories?

3. Talk about the relationship of physical idols to demonic spirits.
4. When Doris Wagner saw the spirit in her bedroom, she first experienced fear, then anger. Can you identify with such emotions?
5. Discuss both sides of not seeing demons at all and seeing too many of them.

Notes
1. George Schwab, ed., *Tribes of the Liberian Hinterland* (Cambridge, MA: Report of the Peabody Museum Expedition to Liberia, 1947), p. 163.
2. This case study is taken from a paper, "Demons and Idols," written by Richard Collingridge while studying at Fuller Seminary in April 1986.
3. Roy Rosedale, "Mobil Training Centers: Key to Growth in Thailand," *Evangelical Missions Quarterly*, October 1989, pp. 402-409.
4. Paul Eshleman, *I Just Saw Jesus* (San Bernardino, CA: Campus Crusade for Christ, 1985), p. 112.
5. Ibid.
6. This hypothesis was previously published in my chapter "Territorial Spirits" in *Wrestling with Dark Angels*, edited by C. Peter Wagner and F. Douglas Pennoyer (Ventura, CA: Regal Books, 1990), p. 77.
7. George Eldon Ladd, *A Theology of the New Testament* (Grand Rapids, MI: Wm. B. Eerdmans Publishing Company, 1974), pp. 400-401.
8. Leon Morris, *The First Epistle of Paul to the Corinthians: An Introduction and Commentary* (Grand Rapids, MI: Wm. B. Eerdmans Publishing Company, 1958), p. 147.
9. Leland Webb, "Spiritual Warfare: Reports from the Front," *The Commission*, February-March 1991, p. 30.
10. David W. Shenk and Ervin R. Stutzman, *Creating Communities of the Kingdom* (Scottdale, PA: Herald Press, 1988), p. 69.
11. Michael Harper, *Spiritual Warfare* (London, England: Hodder and Stoughton, 1970), p. 106.
12. Dom Robert Petipierre, ed., *Exorcism: The Report of a Commission Convened by the Bishop of Exeter* (London, England: S.P.C.K., 1972), p. 9.
13. Ibid., pp. 21-22.
14. Vivienne Stacey, "The Practice of Exorcism and Healing," *Muslims and Christians on the Emmaus Road*, J. Dudley Woodberry, ed. (Monrovia, CA: MARC, 1989), pp. 298-300.
15. James Marocco, "Territorial Spirits," a research paper written in Fuller Theological Seminary, 1988, p. 5.
16. Don Crawford, *Miracles in Indonesia* (Wheaton, IL: Tyndale House Publishers, 1972), p. 144.
17. C. S. Lewis, *The Screwtape Letters* (New York, NY: Macmillan, 1962), p. 3.

Territoriality Then and Now

CHAPTER FIVE

THE BOOK OF REVELATION CONTAINS THE MOST SUSTAINED account of strategic-level spiritual warfare in the Bible. As the drama builds, a powerful demonic being appears as a harlot. She is such a fierce enemy of the gospel that she is drunk—drunk with the blood of persecuted and martyred Christians.

Quite notably, the apostle John, who by this stage of his revelatory vision had virtually seen it all, "marveled with great amazement" when he saw her (Rev. 17:6). She must have been awesome.

This harlot of Revelation 17 is in all probability the most influential territorial spirit mentioned in Scripture. For one thing she, apparently habitually, had engaged in sexual relations and become one flesh with earthly political leaders, "kings of the earth." Whether this connotes literal succubus we are not told, but the language does not exclude the possibility.

We are told that this obscene evil creature "sits on many waters" (Rev. 17:1). What are these waters? "The waters which you saw,...are peoples, multitudes, nations, and tongues" (Rev. 17:15). Here we have an explicit reference to an evil supernatural being who had gained the highest level of malicious control over human social networks of many kinds. I have been calling this sort of being a territorial spirit.

SPIRITS AND TERRITORIES

The notion that spirits are assigned to geographical areas, cultural groups, nations, cities or, as the Bishop of Exeter's report says, "countrysides," has not up to now received much notice or attracted much scholarly attention. I recently took the pains to examine every book in the Fuller Seminary library listed in the card catalog under "angelology" and "demonology" to see how many of these authors dealt with territoriality. Of the 100 books I perused, only 5 of them made any reference at all to territories, and of the 5 only 3 discussed the issues a bit, but clearly in a secondary way.

As I continued to research, I did find bits and pieces from various authors in out-of-print books, periodicals, research papers, sections in other books, and other sources, most of which are not in the seminary library. I put 19 of these together in a book, *Engaging the Enemy* (Regal Books), which many are finding helpful. Interest in the matter of territoriality seems to be escalating rapidly, at least in the circles I am in touch with.

Yale professor, Susan Garrett, who approaches the subject not so much as a spiritual warrior but as a biblical scholar, summarizes her findings in *The Demise of the Devil*, a book I have mentioned previously, by saying that darkness lies like a shroud over the world in which the New Testament was written. "The dark regions are the realm of Satan, the ruler of this world, who for eons has sat entrenched and well-guarded, his many possessions gathered like trophies around him. The sick and possessed are held captive by his demons; the Gentiles, too, are subject to his dominion, giving him honor and glory that ought to be offered to God."[1] Not only does she mention Gentiles as a specific people group, but she also explains that "Luke believes that there are entire populations of humans who have long been under Satan's authority, willingly giving him glory and obeying his command."[2]

More and more people these days are interested in finding out what all of this means, particularly as it might apply to both world evangelization and improvement of human society. I believe it will be helpful to look a bit more closely at territoriality *then*, in the Old Testament and the New Testament, and *now* from the point of view of contemporary anthropologists and missiologists.

OLD TESTAMENT TERRITORIALITY

Throughout the Old Testament, it is evident that the peoples of that day—unfortunately including Israel at certain times—regarded gods, deities, spirits or angelic powers of various kinds as having territorial jurisdiction. A prominent example is the fierce dislike Jehovah God had for high places. Texts such as Numbers 33:52, which commands the children of Israel to "destroy all their engraved stones, destroy all their molded images, and demolish all their high places" are too numerous to catalog. As I pointed out in the last chapter, there was more to these stones and images and high places than just harmless native art. Many of these had become the literal dwelling place of demonic spirits, later in the New Testament called principalities and powers.

Some of the fiercest expressions of God's anger are connected with Israelites who, rather than destroy the high places, worshiped and served the demonic beings that occupied them.

Ahaz was one who "in every single city of Judah he made high places to burn incense to other gods, and provoked to anger the Lord God of his fathers" (2 Chron. 28:25). The result? "They were the ruin of him and of all Israel" (2 Chron. 28:23). Time after time God had to execute judgment and punish Israel for what was frequently referred to by the prophets as spiritual adultery. The Babylonian captivity was one such judgment.

THE PENTATEUCH

The Pentateuch provides us with one of the key texts for understanding the territoriality of spirit beings. It is part of the Song of Moses in Deuteronomy 32:8. Unfortunately, its meaning is hidden in most English versions translated from the Hebrew of the Masoretic text. For example, my *New King James Version* says:

> When the Most High divided their inheritance to the
> nations,
> When He separated the sons of Adam,
> He set the boundaries of the peoples
> According to the number of the *children of Israel.*

The problem comes with the phrase, "children of Israel," which would in itself have little to do with spirits ruling territories. However, biblical scholars such as F. F. Bruce tell us that, due to some discoveries from the Dead Sea scrolls in Cave 4 at Qumram, we now know that the Septuagint version, which is the Greek translation of the Hebrew made about 250 years before the birth of Christ, more accurately represents the original text. Instead of saying that God set the boundaries of people groups according to the number of the children of Israel, it informs us that He set them "according to the number of the angels of God." A crucial difference, to say the least.

F. F. Bruce says, "This reading implies that the administration of various nations has been parcelled out among a corresponding number of angelic powers." He then goes on to elaborate by carrying the implications of this to Daniel 10 where the "prince of Persia" and the "prince of Greece" are mentioned. He further ties it to the New Testament by saying, "In a number of places some at least of these angelic governors are portrayed as hostile principalities and powers—the 'world-rulers of this darkness' of Ephesians 6:12."[3]

Moving back from Moses to Abraham, we receive further light on spiritual territoriality in Old Testament times. In analyzing the spiritual context of Ur of the Chaldees and the Sumerian civilization from which Abraham was called by God, biblical scholar Don Williams points out that the Sumerians were dominated by a "pantheon of gods" and "centralized rule was seen as their gift, making life possible." A territorial spirit named *Enlil* headed up the divine hierarchy, but he ruled in consultation with a heavenly council. "Each city was the property of its god, and its citizens were its slaves." Abraham was the first among them to understand that Jehovah was king of the whole universe.[4] The difference between God and territorial spirits was beginning to come clear.

HISTORICAL BOOKS

Israel was at war with Syria (Aram) almost 900 years before Christ. Ben-Hadad, the Syrian king, was planning military strategy. His advisors told him that the gods of the Israelites were gods of the hills, while the gods of the Syrians were gods of the plains. Therefore, he should arrange it so the battle would take place on the plains (see 1 Kings 20:23). This shows that the Syrians perceived ruling spirits to have, if not territoriality, at least topographical jurisdiction. Nothing in the passage or elsewhere in the Old Testament contradicts their perception of territorial spirits ruling areas. The assumption is that they were correct. Their big error was that they wrongly considered Jehovah God as just another territorial spirit.

This is why Jehovah raised up a prophet at that time to speak to Ahab, king of Israel. God said through the prophet, "Because the Syrians have said, 'The Lord is God of the hills, but He is not God of the valleys,' therefore I will deliver all

---

Much of the Old Testament is based on the assumption that certain supernatural spiritual beings have dominion over geo-political spheres.

---

this great multitude into your hand, and you shall know that I am the Lord" (1 Kings 20:28). When the battle started, it turned out to be a one-day war! The outnumbered Israelites killed 100,000 Syrian troops in that single day, demonstrating dramatically that Jehovah was Lord of hills, of valleys and for that matter of the entire universe.

One of the most detailed treatments of the territorial nature of the pagan so-called gods is found in 2 Kings 17. Israel was in very bad shape spiritually. "They built for themselves high places in all their cities" (2 Kings 17:9), they were setting up "sacred pillars and wooden images on every high hill and under every green tree" (2 Kings 17:10), and they provoked the Lord to anger because "they served idols, of which the Lord had said to them, 'You shall not do this thing'" (2 Kings 17:12). As if this weren't bad enough, they "worshiped all the host of heaven," served Baal, sacrificed their children to the fire god, and practiced witchcraft (see 2 Kings 17:16,17). God reacted decisively "and removed them from His sight" (2 Kings 17:18), and then the Assyrians moved into their land with settlers from many nations.

The new immigrants also imported their spirits and they manufactured appropriate images and shrines to personify them. The spirits had specific names. We are told that those from Babylon made *Succoth Benoth*, those from Cuth made *Nergal*, those of Hamath made *Ashima*, the Avites made *Nibhaz* and *Tartak*, and the Sepharvites burned their children in fire to *Adrammelech* and *Anammelech* (see 2 Kings 17:29-31). There is little question that each people group perceived itself to be under the direct influence of a specific principality whose name and habits they well knew, and to whom they were sub-servient.

THE PROPHETS

In a word from Jeremiah the prophet against Babylon and the land of the Chaldeans, God declared, "Babylon is taken, Bel is shamed. Merodach is broken in pieces; her idols are humiliat-ed, her images are broken in pieces" (Jer. 50:2,3). The word "Bel" or "Baal" is a generic name for "Lord," and here it is applied to *Merodach*, as in *Lord Merodach*. He was "the state-god of Babylon"[5] or the ranking territorial spirit over that nation.

In chapter 3 I mentioned the enlightening passage in Daniel 10 where specifically the "prince of Persia" and the "prince of Greece" are named. It will not be necessary here to recount the details, but simply to reiterate the concept of territoriality. Old Testament scholars Keil and Delitzsch conclude that the "prince of Persia" is indeed the demon of the Persian kingdom. They refer to him as "the supernatural spiritual power standing behind the national gods, which we may properly call the guardian spirit of the kingdom."[6]

In summary, it does seem that, without providing a great

amount of detail, much of the Old Testament is based on the assumption that certain supernatural spiritual beings have dominion over geo-political spheres. Not only that, but it is important to note that these concepts carried through the intertestamental time to the Jewish people of New Testament times. Oscar Cullmann says, "This abundantly attested late Jewish belief that all peoples are ruled through angels is present particularly in *The Book of Daniel*, in *The Wisdom of Jesus, Son of Sirach*, and in the *Book of Enoch*, and it can be shown to be present also in the *Talmud* and *Midrash*...The existing earthly political power belongs in the realm of such angelic powers."[7]

THE NEW TESTAMENT

I began this chapter by citing the harlot of Revelation 17, which is the most explicit New Testament example I have found of a demonic spirit controlling nations and peoples. Susan Garrett, in her detailed study of Luke's writings, concludes that "Luke regards Satan as a powerful being with much of the world under his authority. He controls individuals by means of sickness and demon possession. He controls entire kingdoms, whose inhabitants live in the darkness of idolatry, worshipping Satan and giving him the glory that is due God alone."[8] That Satan controls kingdoms is also obvious from the offer he made Jesus at the temptation in the wilderness when he showed Jesus all the kingdoms of the world and said, "All these things I will give You if You will fall down and worship me" (Matt. 4:9).

THE PRINCIPALITIES AND POWERS

For decades, dating back to World War II and the Nazi atrocities, theologians have argued with each other about the implications of Ephesians 6:12: "We do not wrestle against flesh and blood, but against principalities, against powers." Just how do spiritual principalities and powers relate to everyday flesh and blood such as nations or human governments? Could it be there really are spiritual forces directing human affairs? If so, what is their nature? Some of the more prominent names associated with the debate are G.B. Caird, Markus Barth, Heinrich Schlier, Richard Mouw, John Howard Yoder, Hendrik Berkhof and oth-

---

Social structures, like demonized human beings, can be delivered from demonic oppression through warfare prayer....history belongs to the intercessors.

---

ers. One of the most influential these days is Walter Wink.

Although Walter Wink and I might not see eye to eye on the exact nature of these spiritual forces, we do agree something evil is operating through society that cannot be explained simply by analyzing human nature, depraved as it might be, or by the application of sociological principles. He argues that the early Christians perceived "every nation and tribe and tongue and people" was "presided over by a spiritual Power."[9]

Wink cites, as I have done, Deuteronomy 32:8,9 and Daniel 10, which, as he says, "provides the Bible's fullest picture of these angels and of the nations."[10] Although he doesn't use the term "warfare prayer," he agrees that prayer is our major spiritual weapon, affirming, "This new element in prayer—the resistance of the Powers to God's will—marks a decisive break with the notion that God is the cause of all that happens...Prayer changes us, but it also changes what is possible for God."[11] One of his classic statements is that "History belongs to the intercessors."[12] I couldn't agree more.

As to the nature of the powers, Wink does not believe they are heavenly, transcendent beings, but rather, "the actual inner spirituality of the social entity itself."[13] Ronald J. Sider of Eastern Baptist Seminary sees the powers referring "*both* to the sociopolitical structures of human society *and* to unseen spiritual forces that undergird, lie behind, and in some mysterious way help shape human sociopolitical structures."[14] While deeply respecting the work of these scholars, and while agreeing with their desire to unmask the invisible powers behind the visible structures, I have made clear so far that I hold the position that the principalities and powers are, to be very specific, evil spirits or demons.

I agree with Leon Morris who affirms that we cannot clearly see Paul's conception of Christ's saving work "unless we see it against a background of the evil and the futility in this world, a world populated by evil spirits as well as evil people."[15]

By saying this I want to affirm my agreement with Wink and Sider and others that social structures themselves can properly be seen as demonized. But to my way of thinking they are simply the visible entities, which the invisible demonic forces are using for their own ends much as demonic forces will use an idol, although the idol itself is simply a piece of wood or stone.

A person who is demonized is not per se a demonic person, but rather a victim of a powerful demonic force. Likewise, social structures are not, in themselves, demonic, but they can be and often are demonized by some extremely pernicious and dominating demonic personalities, which I call territorial spirits.

The view I am advocating at least permits a theology of hope. It opens up the possibility that social structures, like demonized human beings, can be delivered from demonic oppression through warfare prayer. This is why I believe that history belongs to the intercessors.

ARTEMIS OF THE EPHESIANS

A case could be made that Paul's power encounter with the sorcerer Bar-Jesus, or Elymas on Cyprus involved a territorial spirit. But the spirit is unnamed and there is nothing specific in the text that would either force such a conclusion or deny it (see Acts 13:6-12). Such is also the situation when Paul cast the spirit of divination out of the slave girl in Philippi (see Acts 16:16-24). I have a strong suspicion that it was a territorial spirit, but no conclusive proof.

The story of Paul's ministry in Ephesus is different. Here we do have the name of the ruling spirit, *Diana* (her Roman name) or *Artemis* (her Greek name) of the Ephesians. Talbot School of Theology's Clinton E. Arnold is a New Testament scholar who has specialized in the book of Ephesians and who helps us see the spiritual warfare implications of the epistle. He laments, "Few N.T. scholars have referred to the Artemis cult as relevant to the background of Ephesians, much less as relevant to the teaching on the hostile 'powers'."[16] He feels that attempting to understand the principalities and powers in Ephesians apart from the cult of Artemis is a mistake.

One reason I agree with Arnold is that leaders of the city of Ephesus itself became so upset by the ministry of the apostle Paul that they feared the goddess Diana's temple would be despised and her magnificence destroyed (see Acts 19:27). They boasted that "all Asia and the world" worships her (v. 27). The city clerk proclaimed, "Who does not know that the city of the Ephesians is temple guardian of the great goddess Diana, and of the image which fell down from Zeus?" (Acts 19:35). Clinton Arnold's historical research confirms that Artemis was worshiped in Colossae, Laodicea, Hierapolis and throughout Asia.

Artemis' power was awesome. Arnold says, "One undisputed characteristic of the Ephesian Artemis is the unsurpassed cosmic power attributed to her." He says that because of her supra-natural powers "she could intercede between her followers and the cruel fate which plagued them." They called her "Savior," "Lord" and "Queen of the Cosmos." She wore the signs of the zodiac around her neck and "possessed an authority and power superior to that of astrological fate."[17]

RELEASING EVANGELISTIC POWER

I believe we will not be too far from wrong if we regard Artemis of the Ephesians as a territorial spirit and see the possible relationship that weakening her had to do with the evangelization of the territory she dominated. Certainly the "word of the Lord grew mightily and prevailed" in Ephesus (Acts 19:20). Not only did a strong church develop there, but Ephesus became an evangelistic center for the whole region to the extent "that all who dwelt in Asia heard the word of the Lord Jesus, both Jews and Greeks" (Acts 19:10).

Some historical sources of the times, other than the Bible, also reveal the belief early Christians had about Artemis. Arnold quotes from *The Acts of Andrew,* which speaks of a crowd of demons in a rock beside a statue of Artemis.[18]

Yale historian Ramsay MacMullen sees much of the Christianization of the Roman Empire as a power encounter between Christianity and the resident demonic forces. He tells the story of one such power encounter involving Artemis from *The Acts of John.* Supposedly the apostle John, unlike the apostle Paul, went into Artemis' temple itself to do strategic-level spiritual warfare. He reportedly prayed the following warfare prayer: "O God...at whose name every idol takes flight and every demon and every unclean power, now let the demon that is here take flight in Thy name." At that moment, so the story goes, the altar of Artemis split in pieces, and half of the temple building collapsed![19]

History again indicates this had a direct evangelistic effect.

The Acts of John records that, following this power encounter led by John, the Ephesians said, "We are converted now that we have seen thy marvellous works." Clinton Arnold's study indicates, "The influx and expansion of Christianity eventually wrought the demise of the cult of the Ephesian Artemis."[20]

TERRITORIALITY NOW: ANTHROPOLOGY

As the field of cultural anthropology has developed in our century, an increasing number of social scientists, both Christian and non-Christian, are realizing it is not possible to fully understand the life-style, values, and behavior patterns of vast segments of the world's population without coming to terms with their supernaturalistic worldview. Fuller Seminary anthropologist Charles H. Kraft has helped us understand this well in his remarkable book, *Christianity with Power*.

Kraft argues that we Westerners divide the world into "natural" and "supernatural" and then proceed to disregard the supernatural. Even as Christians, he says, "We do claim to assume that God is involved in all of our everyday activities. And yet we often base our thinking and behavior on naturalistic assumptions almost as much as do our non-Christian neighbors and friends."[21] This tends to cloud our understanding of the great majority of the peoples of the world for whom the supernatural is very much a part of daily life.

Jacob Loewen is both an anthropologist and a Bible translation consultant. He sees the Old Testament as clearly assuming the territoriality of demonic spirits, frequently called "deities." He cites the prophet Hosea, among others, who continually reprimanded Israel for thinking like the pagans and regarding Jehovah as a territorial spirit instead of the sovereign Lord of the whole universe. Then he says, "The situation described in Hosea is very similar to the situation which we described for Africa where the conquerors felt obliged to accept the gods of the conquered because the latter's deities controlled the land."[22]

Loewen reports that in Central and South America spirits are considered to be the "owners" of geographical or topographical phenomena. Nomadic Indians never travel from one territory to another without first securing the permission of the territorial spirit dominating the area they are about to enter. "People never own the land," Loewen says, "they only use it by the permission of its true spirit owners who, in a sense, 'adopt' them."[23]

When anthropologist David Lan began to study guerilla warfare in Zimbabwe, he soon discovered it was closely related to the activity of spirit mediums. These mediums were possessed by the *mhondoro*, spirits purportedly of dead chiefs. He found that each of these *mhondoro* "is thought to rule over a specific territory which he is believed to have conquered or been given when he was alive." He calls them "spirit provinces." He says of the region he was researching, "Every square centimeter is part of one spirit province or another."[24] While, as a secular anthropologist, he makes no attempt at biblical applications, Lan at least furnishes us with some basis for believing that spiritual mapping may have validity for social science as well as for world evangelization.

TERRITORIALITY IN SOUTHERN MEXICO

One of the finest case studies of spiritual territoriality in a field missionary setting comes from Vernon J. Sterk, who has served with the Reformed Church of America for more than 20 years among the Tzotzil Indians in southern Mexico. He says that every one of the Tzotzil tribes can identify specific, tribal deities by name. They also know the names of evil spirits who are assigned to various kinds of evil activities. They know, for example, that *Yajval Balamil* controls sickness, *Poslom* attacks people with swelling at night, and *J'ic'aletic* are looters and rapists.[25]

Sterk says that both evil spirits and guardian spirits among the Tzotzil "have territorial designations and assignments," and he observes, "All of the spirits have geographical limits for their power, even though the reach of the evil spirits seems to be more extensive than that of the guardian or ancestral spirits."[26] When the territorial spirit is strong, newly converted Christians frequently are forced to move out. Many Tzotzil Indians will not leave their territory because they fear losing the protection of their guardian spirit who cannot leave with them.

Vernon Sterk represents a rapidly growing number of thoughtful field missionaries who are beginning to see that the real battle for the evangelization of their regions is a spiritual battle. While lamenting that he had never been trained in strategic-level spiritual warfare, he nevertheless is looking to the future rather than to the past, and believing that warfare prayer will make a difference in the spiritual harvest among the Tzotzil.

He also speaks for many of us when he, quite honestly, says, "I wish that I could report that we have taken authority over these spirits in Jesus' name and the growth has become fantastic. But neither we who are missionaries nor the expelled Zinacanteco Christians had ever considered this concept of specific territorial spirits. We never did more than pray general prayers against Satan's power in Nabenchauc, and the growth of the church has been generally slow and halting."[27]

My desire is that Vern Sterk and thousands of missionaries and evangelists like him, who have a heart that beats for world evangelization, will learn how to do warfare prayer in a way that will make a measurable difference in the spread of the Kingdom of God throughout the earth.

■ REFLECTION QUESTIONS ■

1. Does it seem strange to you that theologians in the past have not paid much attention to territorial spirits? Why?
2. This chapter gives several examples of known spirits over certain areas in Old Testament times. How many more examples can you name?
3. What was the problem behind the Israelites seeing Jehovah God as a territorial spirit? Is there any danger of that today?
4. Do you think social structures such as governments or industries can be demonized? What examples could you give from your knowledge or experience?
5. Do you feel that the information anthropologists uncover among different peoples has validity? Do some so-called "primitive" people know more about the spirit world than most of us do?

Notes

1. Susan R. Garrett, *The Demise of the Devil* (Minneapolis, MN: Fortress Press, 1989), p. 101.
2. Ibid., p. 40.
3. F.F. Bruce, *The Epistle to the Hebrews* (Grand Rapids, MI: Wm. B. Eerdmans Publishing Co., 1964), p. 33.
4. Don Williams, *Signs, Wonders and the Kingdom of God* (Ann Arbor, MI: Vine Books, Servant Publications, 1989), p. 35.
5. *Interpreter's Dictionary of the Bible* (Nashville, TN: Abingdon Press, 1962), Vol. 1, p. 376.
6. C.F. Keil, *Biblical Commentary on the Book of Daniel* (Grand Rapids, MI: Wm. B. Eerdmans Publishing Co., 1949), p. 416.
7. Oscar Cullmann, "The Subjection of the Invisible Powers," *Engaging the Enemy*, C. Peter Wagner, ed. (Ventura, CA: Regal Books, 1991), p. 195.
8. Garrett, *The Demise of the Devil*, p. 43.
9. Walter Wink, *Unmasking the Powers* (Philadelphia, PA: Fortress Press, 1986), p. 88.
10. Ibid., p. 89.
11. Ibid., p. 91.
12. Walter Wink, "Prayer and the Powers," *Sojourners*, October 1990, p. 10.
13. Wink, *Unmasking the Powers*, p. 88.
14. Ronald J. Sider, *Christ and Violence* (Scottdale, PA: Herald Press, 1979), p. 50.
15. Leon Morris, *New Testament Theology* (Grand Rapids, MI: Academie Books, Zondervan Publishing House, 1986), p. 66.

16. Clinton E. Arnold, *Ephesians: Power and Magic* (Cambridge, England: Cambridge University Press, 1989), p. 27.

17. Ibid., p. 21.

18. Ibid., p. 27.

19. Ramsay MacMullen, *Christianizing the Roman Empire, A.D. 100-400* (New Haven, CT: Yale University Press, 1984), p. 26.

20. Arnold, *Ephesians*, p. 28.

21. Charles H. Kraft, *Christianity with Power* (Ann Arbor, MI: Vine Books, Servant Publications, 1989), p. 27.

22. Jacob Loewen, "Which God Do Missionaries Preach?" *Engaging the Enemy*, C. Peter Wagner, ed. (Ventura, CA: Regal Books, 1991), p. 173.

23. Ibid., p. 169.

24. David Lan, *Guns and Rain: Guerillas and Spirit Mediums in Zimbabwe* (Berkeley: University of California Press, 1985), p. 34.

25. Vernon J. Sterk, "Territorial Spirits and Evangelization in Hostile Environments," *Engaging the Enemy*, C. Peter Wagner, ed. (Ventura, CA: Regal Books, 1991), p. 149.

26. Ibid, pp. 149-150.

27. Ibid., pp. 155-156.

Equipping the Warriors

CHAPTER SIX

WHEN YOUNG PEOPLE ENLIST IN THE MARINES, THEIR first stop is boot camp. There they receive intensive, basic training geared to carry them across the threshold from civilian to military life. The major purpose of boot camp is to develop the character that will sustain a Marine in the crisis situations of battle. This is partially done through grueling physical disciplines designed to build both muscle and stamina. But even more important is the psychological conditioning necessary to assure that every Marine believes in the mission of the Marine Corps, develops courage and self-discipline, and is fully prepared to submit to authority and obey commands with no questions asked.

Without the basic training of boot camp, Marines would never win a battle, much less a war.

SPIRITUAL BOOT CAMP

Basic training applies equally to Christians who desire to do spiritual warfare. Too many Christians want to get involved in the action without first submitting themselves to the discipline necessary to equip a warrior for battle. To the degree that they do, they leave themselves open to serious personal attack and they run the risk of bringing discredit to the Body of Christ.

Spiritual warfare should be seen as involving two simultaneous movements: the upward and the outward. Some call them Godward and Satanward. In a book that has become a Christian classic, *Quiet Talks on Prayer*, S. D. Gordon, at around the turn of the last century, pointed out that "prayer concerns three." It first concerns God to whom we pray, then the person doing the praying, but also the evil one against whom we pray. "The purpose of prayer," says Gordon, "is not to persuade or influence God, but to join forces with him against the enemy." Joining with God against Satan is essential in prayer. "The real pitch is not Godward, but Satanward," Gordon says.[1]

Although our goal in spiritual warfare is to join God in defeating the enemy, we must never forget that we, in ourselves, have no power to defeat him. "Not by might nor by power, but by My Spirit, says the Lord of hosts" (Zech. 4:6). The principle here is that it is extremely dangerous to attempt to move too far outward without first moving far enough upward. Moving upward is the spiritual boot camp, while moving outward is the battle. Just as in the Marines, the battle cannot be won without first going through boot camp.

I find it helpful to conceptualize what I am saying by using a simple diagram. I have arbitrarily numbered the upward and the outward scales from 1 to 10. Although these numbers are very subjective, the best advice I can give in spiritual warfare is at all times to make sure you are scoring higher on the upward scale than on the outward scale.

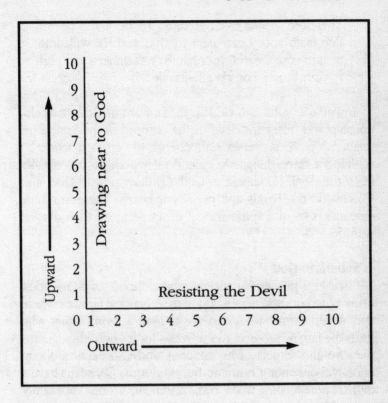

This chapter is about the upward side of the diagram, our personal, spiritual basic training. The rest of the book will describe in some detail our battle plan and what it means to move Satanward. But the sequence cannot be changed. We must look at the Godward side first.

JAMES TELLS US HOW

A central text for understanding the relationship of the upward to the outward is James 4:7,8:

> Therefore submit to God. Resist the devil and he will
> flee from you. Draw near to God and He will draw
> near to you. Cleanse your hands, you sinners; and puri-
> fy your hearts, you double-minded.

In verse 7 "submit to God" is the upward or Godward relationship and "resist the devil" is the outward or the Satanward
relationship. These verses elaborate on the upward action by
setting out three things we must do if we are to successfully
resist the devil: (1) submit to God; (2) draw near to God; and
(3) cleanse our hands and purify our hearts. These are three
essential parts of a spiritual boot camp designed to equip the
warriors.

1. Submit to God

We live in a permissive society where almost anything goes.
Many of today's adults grew up in dysfunctional families where
they never learned what it means to have a loving father who
leads the family, protects and provides for his household, earns
the love and respect of his children, and also expects obedience. Not only non-Christians, but even some Christians have a
difficult time relating to the commandment, "Honor your father
and mother" and the biblical admonition: "Children, obey your
parents in the Lord, for this is right" (Eph. 6:1). Rebellion often
seems to be a more popular attitude today than loyalty.

Christians who never willingly submitted to a natural father
frequently find it difficult to submit to their heavenly Father.
They seek God for love, gentleness, forgiveness and healing
but draw back from God's demands for obedience and commitment. They have never fully come to terms with the concept
that "Jesus is Lord." In first-century society when the New Testament was written, there was no doubt in anyone's mind that
a lord was to be obeyed without question. Christians who are
not ready to obey God unconditionally are no more ready for

spiritual warfare than Marines who are not ready to obey their commanding officers.

The Bible uses some very strong language when it deals with obedience. How do we know that we know God? "Now by this we know that we know Him, if we keep His commandments" (1 John 2:3). The New Testament does not allow the false separation of loving God on the one hand and submitting to Him as master on the other, which many believers

---

Our personal prayer life is the principal barometer used to measure the quality of our relationship to God.

---

these days wish might be true. It clearly says, "For this is the love of God, that we keep His commandments" (1 John 5:3).

Submitting to God is the first lesson of spiritual boot camp.

2. Draw Near to God

Drawing near to God is the second lesson. This has to do with our personal prayer life. Prayer in general is a broad subject with many extremely important facets. But none is more important for a Christian who desires to do effective spiritual warfare than personal prayer.

Why is personal prayer that important?

Our personal prayer life is the principal barometer used to measure the quality of our relationship to God. I agree with John Wimber when he says, "Intimacy with God in prayer is a primary goal of the Christian life." Jesus provides our example. The world knew that Jesus was authentic because Jesus did only what He saw the Father doing (John 5:19). Wimber asks, "Why is our goal intimacy with God?" His perceptive answer is that only in sustaining a close relationship with the Father "do we experience forgiveness, renewal, and power for righteous living. Only in an intimate relationship with God can we hear His voice, know His will, understand His heart."[2]

Like it or not, drawing near to God requires time. If we are motivated to pray, the first and most important act of self-discipline for implementation is to set aside blocks of clock time. Once you budget the time, a kind of spiritual Parkinson's law comes into play and prayer tends to expand to fill the time available. Those who do not carve out time, particularly those who rationalize their reluctance to do so by claiming "I pray without ceasing," usually end up praying very little.

One reason some do not dedicate much time to prayer is that they don't enjoy it. My daughter Ruth hated to wash dishes when she was at home. I was amused to observe through the years that by far the most urgent and critical demand on her time invariably came immediately after we finished dinner. Since she hated to wash dishes, there was always some higher priority demand on her time.

Many Christians have the same attitude toward personal prayer. There always seems to be something more urgent to do. Time for prayer is scarce because other activities have higher priority. Some even make the statement that "prayer is hard work." I have a difficult time understanding this if the essence of prayer truly is a relationship of intimacy with the Father. It would be like me saying, "Spending time with my wife, Doris, is hard work." I would never say that for two reasons. First, it is not hard work, it is pure joy. Secondly, if I did say it, she would take it as an insult, and I wouldn't blame her. Could it be that God might take such an attitude as an insult also?

Enjoying Prayer. How can personal prayer become more enjoyable?

I plan on writing more about personal prayer in another

book in this series on prayer, but because developing strong personal prayer habits is so essential to preparing spiritual warriors for battle, I will briefly mention five principles that will help a great deal if you want to enjoy prayer more:

• *The place*. Find a comfortable, peaceful place as your habitual place of prayer. Having a pleasant and familiar environment will bring you more quickly and naturally into an attitude of prayer. To help you relax, take a cup of coffee or a glass of juice with you. There is nothing wrong with feeling good while you are praying.

• *The time*. I agree with Larry Lea that a reasonable long-range goal for a daily prayer time is one hour. I also understand that for many this will be a lifelong goal that may never be reached on a regular basis. If you are starting from scratch, use short-range goals and plan to increase the time gradually. If this sounds quite demanding to you, try starting with 5 minutes, then increase it to 10. In my opinion, 5 minutes every day is much more valuable than 15 minutes every 3 days, even though I would consider either clearly inadequate for strategic-level spiritual warfare.

• *The attitude*. Concentrate on making your prayer time a personal relationship with God. I like what Pastor John Bisagno says: "Prayer is a conversation, a union, an intermingling of two personalities. God speaks to me and I speak to Him." For many of us, it will take some effort and experience to allow this to happen because we are not used to hearing from God. Bisagno says, "Waiting on God is not a mere abstract passing of time. It is a definite spiritual exercise during which, after having spoken to God, He in turn, speaks to you."[3] Few things will make prayer more enjoyable than hearing God speak to you. Some experienced pray-ers even take notes on what He says and call it "journaling."

• *The format*. I strongly suggest using the Lord's Prayer as a daily format for the entire prayer time. This advice has been frequently given since the time of Martin Luther, but the present day manual I recommend most is Larry Lea's *Could You Not Tarry One Hour?* (Creation House).

• *The quality*. Experience shows that the quality of prayer usually follows the quantity, not vice versa. As you develop a personal prayer life, do not be overconcerned with sleepiness or daydreaming. Quality will come over time. I once heard Mike Bickel say that if you set aside 60 minutes for prayer you may begin by getting 5 good minutes. But then the 5 become 10, the 10 become 20 and the quality increases.

Enjoying prayer is a sure sign that you are receiving good preparation for spiritual warfare.

Fasting. From time to time, when Jesus' disciples ran into trouble trying to cast out a demon, Jesus had to instruct them that certain kinds come out only through prayer and fasting (see Matt. 17:21). Just as it is necessary for us to draw near to God through prayer, it is also necessary to draw near through fasting. Learning how to fast is part of spiritual boot camp.

Many who read this will be experienced, practicing fasters. This short section is not for you, but for those who are wondering how to begin. Although there are many different kinds of fasts, the most common, and the one I recommend for starting, is to abstain from food, but not drink, for a given period of time. So far as drink is concerned, all agree that water is basic. Some add coffee or tea, some add fruit juices. All also agree that something like a milk shake goes too far, and is not in the spirit of fasting. Whatever, the fast involves an intentional practice of self-denial, and this spiritual discipline has been known through the centuries as a means for opening ourselves to God and drawing closer to Him.

I think fasting should be practiced both on a regular basis and also occasionally as needed or as agreed. I myself am just a beginner, so I have decided to discipline myself not to eat anything between Tuesday supper and Wednesday noon. This, I have found, is not hard to do. The hardest part was to decide to do it. This is my regular fast, and it has taken any reticence about fasting away from me. On this basis, the occasional, longer fasts are much easier. A while ago, for example, I was invited to a retreat where we were to pray and fast all day long, and because of the habit I had developed I had no problem at all.

Sometimes we don't encourage other members of the Body of Christ to fast because we recall Jesus' rebuke to the Pharisees that they sinned by making a public display of fasting (see Matt. 6:16-18). Just because we should fast in secret does not mean, in my opinion, that we should keep fasting a secret or not encourage others to do it by our example. That is why I share my present fasting habits in print here. We need to talk about fasting more and do it more!

To the degree that fasting becomes more of a norm in our day-to-day Christian life as individuals and congregations, we will become more effective in spiritual warfare.

Drawing near to God through prayer and fasting is the second important lesson of spiritual boot camp.

3. Cleanse Your Hands and Purify Your Hearts

In His instructions for submitting to God, Jesus says, "Cleanse your hands, you sinners; and purify your hearts, you double-minded" (Jas. 4:8). Cleansing the hands refers to what you do, and purifying the hearts is what you think or feel. Put together, this is a call to holiness, and holiness includes both attitude and action.

Developing holiness is essential for a spiritual warrior. Unfortunately, various aspects of holiness have been so blown out of biblical proportion in recent times that holiness has become not a blessing for spiritual warfare as God intends it, but a barrier to effective spiritual warfare. This is an important enough aspect of spiritual boot camp training that I feel it needs considerable attention in this chapter.

THE "BLESS ME" TRAP

In August 1990, 25,000 charismatics gathered in the Indianapolis Hoosier Dome for the third largest congress of its kind. Some observers felt the meeting represented a turning point of sorts for the charismatic movement. A *Christianity Today* editorial commented approvingly that this time the charismatics did not gather just for hand raising, fervent praying and exuberant singing as they had in the past. This time they were challenged to move out in aggressive evangelism at home and abroad, especially targeting the poor.

In fact, *Christianity Today* was bold enough to suggest that Indianapolis was an indication that the charismatic movement is "coming of age."[4]

What is it that would cause some evangelicals and others to regard the 30-year-old charismatic movement as less than mature? Vinson Synan, the congress director and chairperson of the sponsoring North American Renewal Service Committee, probably put his finger on it when he said, "This was not a bless me conference."[5]

Synan was comparing the attendance of the 1977 Kansas City conference (50,000) and the 1987 New Orleans conference (35,000) to the 25,000 in Indianapolis. Both Kansas City and New Orleans were regarded by the leadership as "bless me" events. But the theme of Indianapolis was "Evangelize the World—*Now!*" Synan's view is that when the emphasis shifted from bless me to bless them, the interest among charismatics dropped considerably, and so did the attendance.

Charismatics certainly do not hold a corner on the bless me brand of Christianity despite the disproportionately high profile of some rather questionable application of healing and pros-

perity teaching. Countless thousands of non-charismatic churches also suffer severe cases of "koinonitis," which is legitimate
Christian fellowship gone to seed. "Visitors welcome" signs
over the front door of the church mean virtually nothing in all
too many cases. The bless me trap knows no denominational
boundaries.

Churches, of course, *should* bless me. Few people would
attend if there were no personal benefits. Jesus says, "Come to
Me, all you who labor and are heavy laden, and I will give you
rest" (Matt. 11:28). We invite our hurting friends to come to
church with us so they can experience emotional, physical and
spiritual healing. In a real and legitimate sense the church is
seen as a hospital to care for the wounded.

But while the Church rightly functions as a hospital for healing the wounded, it must also be seen as a barracks for the
warriors. It is a place for teaching, training, equipping and spiritual conditioning. It is a place where people are filled with the
Holy Spirit and power not simply to bless me but also to be
witnesses for Jesus in Jerusalem, Judea, Samaria and to the
uttermost parts of the earth. The Church does what healing is
necessary but the primary function of the healing is to build up
the troops for moving out to the front lines in Kingdom ministries of all kinds.

HOLINESS FOR WARFARE

Holiness is as indispensable for a spiritual warrior as is good
eyesight for a military fighter pilot. Most Christian leaders will
agree with this, but some go on to develop the idea of holiness
on a first grade Dick and Jane level. They deal with the milk of
the Word on holiness, but do not seem to get to the meat. And
others, in their commendable desire to emphasize holiness,
tend toward an extreme that would imply holiness is an end in
itself. If God just blesses us with enough holiness, if we con-

centrate on polishing Christians to a high enough luster, effective ministry will supposedly flow forth on its own. This may be somewhat of a caricature, but it is one of the current approaches that can easily lead to the bless me trap. To be effective in spiritual warfare, we need to understand some of the deeper implications of holiness.

Relationships and Rules

The two major facets of Christian holiness are (1) relationships and (2) obedience. Both are prominent in the book of Galatians, a book written for the express purpose of helping Christians live the Christian life in God's way. The churches in Galatia were a mixture of believers from two distinct backgrounds. Some were Jews who had received Jesus as their Messiah. Some were pagans who had received Jesus as their Lord. The Jews knew all about obedience to the law, and Paul had to admonish them not to revert to the idea that keeping the law would in itself please God. "Are you so foolish? Having begun in the Spirit, are you now being made perfect by the flesh?" (Gal. 3:3). The Jews needed to be reminded that the basis of our holiness is our personal relationship to God as children.

The pagans, on the other hand, knew all about relationships to supernatural beings, in their case the principalities, powers and evil spirits. Paul had to admonish them not to turn back to the demonic forces in times of need or crisis. "But now after you have known God, or rather are known by God, how is it that you turn again to the weak and beggarly elements, to which you desire again to be in bondage?" (Gal. 4:9). The pagans needed to be reminded that the basis of our holiness is not only a relationship, but obedience to God as our master.

How, then, are relationships and rules brought together?

I believe the answer to this crucial question becomes clear as we consider three vital aspects of our relationship to God:

1. God is our Father. We begin with a loving relationship to Christ. We are children who say, "Abba, Father!" (Gal. 4:6).

2. God is our master. We have a loving desire to obey Christ's will. We are slaves and we obey, even though we are children. "The heir, as long as he is a child, does not differ at all from a slave" (Gal. 4:1).

3. Jesus is our role model. We want to be Christlike. Paul addressed the Galatian believers as "My little children, for whom I labor in birth again until Christ is formed in you" (Gal. 4:19). Holiness is seeing Christ formed in us.

A relationship of any kind has its demands. My wife, Doris,

> **Holiness is not to love Jesus and do what-ever you want. Holiness is to love Jesus and do what He wants.**

---

and I have maintained a quality relationship for more than 40 years. But it is not maintained automatically. Each of us has our own personality and its accompanying set of standards. We have discovered that our relationship is better if we adhere to each other's standards. The same thing applies to our relationship to Jesus. The sooner we learn the rules and keep them, the better we get along together. The major New Testament passages on holiness such as Ephesians 4:17-32 and Colossians 3:5-24 spell out the rules in some detail. In Galatians, Paul lists both the works of the flesh (Gal. 5:19-21) and the fruit of the Spirit (Gal. 5:22,23).

Holiness is not to love Jesus and do whatever you want. Holiness is to love Jesus and do what He wants. The relationship is basic, but how do we know if we are correctly related to Jesus? "Now by this we know that we know Him, if we keep His commandments" (1 John 2:3).

Who Is Holy?

If holiness is a prerequisite for spiritual warfare, can a person actually be holy? Can I declare that I have attained holiness? If I can't, why do we keep admonishing one another to be holy?

At first, these may sound like confusing questions. But the confusion is cleared up if we ask two questions instead of one. The first question is: Can anyone be holy? The answer is yes. Every Christian is holy. The second question is: Can anyone be holy enough? The answer is no. No Christian is holy enough.

It is important, of course, to make sure we understand what the word "holiness" means. The Greek *hagios* means to be set apart; biblically it means to be set apart for God. It is synonymous to "sanctification." But the biblical emphasis is on the relationship more than the being set apart.

In the sense of being set aside for God, every Christian has been made holy through the new birth. Peter says we are a "holy priesthood" (1 Pet. 2:5) and a "holy nation" (1 Pet. 2:9). Jesus will "present you holy, and blameless, and irreproachable in His sight" (Col. 1:22). Paul reminds the believers in Corinth that "you were sanctified . . . by the Spirit of our God" (1 Cor. 6:11). If you are born again, you can truly say, "Yes, I am holy."

But you cannot say, "I am holy enough." Positionally, as a child of God, you no longer practice sin. "Whoever abides in Him does not sin" (1 John 3:6). But while the desire of your heart as prompted by the Holy Spirit is no longer to practice sin as a life-style, you are not yet perfect. You do, in fact, sin and you might as well admit it. "If we say that we have no sin, we deceive ourselves, and the truth is not in us" (1 John 1:8). This is why Jesus tells us to pray daily, "Forgive us our sins."

Maturing in Holiness

Well, if we can't ever be holy *enough*, can we at least be *more* holy than we were, say, last year? Certainly. I believe I can honestly say that I was more holy in 1990 than I was in 1980. I fully hope, plan and intend to be still more holy 10 years from now. In 20 years, according to actuarial tables, I will probably be holy enough at last, because I will likely be in Jesus' presence!

In their enthusiasm for attaining greater holiness, some have fallen into the temptation Paul was trying to warn the Galatians against. They have selected certain outward actions or experiences as visible tests of the attainment of holiness or sanctification or fullness of the Spirit. Members of some churches knowingly wink at each other and say, "I had my experience in 1986. When did you have yours?"

Some years ago while cutting my hair, a barber told me he had his experience 14 years previously and since then he had never sinned. The accomplishment of outward standards, good as they might be, is not a biblical approach to measuring holiness. Much more important is holiness of heart or inward holiness. The direction one is heading is more significant than outward accomplishments, as Jesus' words to the Pharisees in Matthew 6 clearly indicate.

Reasons for Outward Standards
What good are outward standards? Outward standards help us in our quest for holiness in three ways:

First, we can define the *absence* of holiness by using outward standards. At the same time, we cannot define the *presence* of holiness by compliance with such, as we have just seen. If we habitually use the Lord's name in vain, engage in extramarital sex, and falsify financial reports—to give three examples of outward standards—we can be sure that we are not holy.

Second, outward standards are indicators of maturity. God is a good father—He understands His spiritual children. But He also expects His children to grow up, just as we do our natural children. What parent hasn't said to a child in first grade, "Stop acting like a two-year-old!" Sometimes God has to say that to us. Paul displayed his frustration at the Corinthians when he said with disgust, "I, brethren, could not speak to you as to spiritual people but as to carnal, as to babes in Christ" (1 Cor. 3:1). Keep in mind that this spiritual maturity will be most evident through mature character traits rather than checking off someone's list of rules.

Third, the highest New Testament standards are for leaders. As the requirements for elders and deacons in the pastoral epistles reflect, outward actions and visible, overt, public testimonies are necessary requirements, not for avoiding excommunication from the church, but for qualifying for leadership positions.

How Much Is Enough?

If Christians are never holy enough, but if they can advance in holiness, how far do they need to advance before moving out in ministry? How much refinement do the troops need before they are sent into battle?

In answering these questions, four dangers need to be avoided:

1. Waiting until you are perfect before moving out. This results in ministry paralysis since no one makes it to perfection in this life.
2. Regarding holiness as an end in itself. This results in the bless me syndrome, which so many are trying to avoid these days.
3. Expecting ministry to self-generate from a holy life. This results in the inward journey turning out to be a dead-end street. Ministry requires motivation and initiative regardless of the level of holiness.
4. Relating effectiveness in ministry to compliance with

certain outward indicators of holiness. This results in pride and self-centeredness.

PRINCIPLES FOR WARFARE

Now for the principles. We want to be good spiritual warriors, so we know we must achieve holiness. Yet we want to avoid the bless me trap and ministry paralysis. Here are five principles that will help equip us for battle:

1. Be sure you are in proper relationship to God. The basics are: knowing you are born again, knowing you have a satisfactory personal prayer life and knowing you are filled with the Holy Spirit. Note: This checkpoint is in *proper* relationship to God, not a *perfect* relationship. The crucial test is that your heart desire is to know God more intimately and to please Him in all things.

2. Confess all known sins. Most mature believers know when they have sinned. But just to check periodically, use the list of the works of the flesh in Galatians 5:19-21 and other biblical lists of sins as a starting point. Francis Frangipane warns: "If you attempt to bind a principality or power while you harbor sin in your heart, you will surely be defeated."[6] Note: Do not indulge in spiritual self-flagellation. That is also a work of the flesh. Something is wrong if you do not feel good unless you feel guilty! Allow the Holy Spirit Himself to convict you of sin.

3. Seek healing for persistent sin patterns. If you have a heart for God but a particular sin continues to surface, this is a spiritual illness for which you must seek healing just as you would seek healing for a bladder infection or sugar diabetes. Note: You will usually need outside help for this inner healing. Get the help before you attempt any ministry, but especially before you attempt spiritual warfare.

4. Allow others to read your spiritual barometer. Relate closely to a number of other people whose spirituality you respect and who know you well enough to be frank with you. Note: Too much openness, especially in public, can itself become pathological. But by keeping everything to yourself, you have no way to test the accuracy of your self-evaluations.

5. The higher God calls you to leadership, the higher your standards of holiness. Many levels of Christian ministry are not overly demanding for holiness, although mature holiness is a goal for all believers. Some forms of ministry are like playing touch football with kids on the front lawn. Not too demanding. But other levels of ministry are more like the National Football League, and they require a spiritual conditioning that is considerably above the average. Note: Strategic-level spiritual warfare should be considered more in the NFL category. If you feel you are gifted and called to this kind of ministry, be especially strict with yourself.

If your score on this checklist is satisfactory, you are ready for ministry. Don't separate holy character from giftings or ministry or you will end up with hypocrisy. At the same time, don't wait until you have attained superholiness before you do ministry or you will end up in the bless me trap.

THE WHOLE ARMOR OF GOD

A manual I like for equipping warriors for battle is Larry Lea's *The Weapons of Your Warfare*. In it he lists the blood of Jesus, prayer, the whole armor of God, praise, speaking the Word, the name of Jesus and perseverance as "God's storehouse of spiritual weapons." Space will not permit me to elaborate on all of them here, so I will simply recommend Lea's book as a textbook for your spiritual warfare boot camp.

I do, however, want to mention the whole armor of God before concluding this chapter. In *The Weapons of Your Warfare*, Larry Lea uses the American "dress for success" mentality as an illustration. Many self-help books instruct aspiring business people how certain clothing gives them a "look" that will allow them to move up the business ladder more rapidly. He then goes on to say that putting on the whole armor of God is "the only way to dress for success in the Lord, because the whole armor of God is a prerequisite to taking the Kingdom of God by force."[7]

Paul's metaphor of the armor of the Roman Legionnaire gives us a list of vital elements in the preparation of spiritual warriors. Our loins need to be girded with truth. Jesus Himself is the way, the truth and the life. We put on a breastplate of righteousness. Our heart is protected by the holiness of cleansing our hands and purifying our hearts as we have seen earlier. The shield of faith protects us from Satan's fiery darts. The helmet of salvation reminds us that we belong to Jesus and that we are assured of final victory in the battle.

As I have read extensively in the area of spiritual warfare, I am puzzled by the considerable number of authors who feel the need to make a special point that all the pieces of the armor of God are defensive. The fact is that the warrior not only wears armor and holds a shield, but has a sword in his right hand. The sword of the Spirit, which is the Word of God, is certainly an offensive weapon. I enjoy Walter Wink's comment, "It is humorous to watch the statement bob from scholar to scholar that the weapons here are all 'defensive.' The Pentagon says the same about nuclear missiles."[8]

Some, I believe, want to hope against hope that since Christ has defeated Satan on the cross, all we are expected to do is to "stand." If we stand around with our hands in our pockets, evil will somehow not bother us or our society. But this is not what Paul had in mind when he wrote Ephesians 6, in my opinion. Clinton Arnold raises the question whether "to stand" is static or dynamic. He asks, "Is the reader also called upon to take more 'offensive' action such as in proclaiming the redemptive message of the gospel to humanity held in bondage by the devil?"

His conclusion is, "The flow of the context also reveals that the author conceives of 'standing' in offensive terms."[9]

Using the whole armor of God, then, we are ready not only to protect ourselves from Satan's onslaughts, but also to overcome the strong man and advance the Kingdom of God.

■ REFLECTION QUESTIONS ■

1. Discuss the upward and outward scale. Explain in your own words what this means.
2. If you were to give yourself a test on submitting to God and drawing near to God, what grade would you give yourself?
3. Do you agree that Christians should shoot for one hour a day in personal prayer, or is this unrealistic?
4. Do you have any experience with fasting? If so, describe it and discuss it.
5. Are you more holy than you used to be? How do you know?

Notes

1. S. D. Gordon, *Quiet Talks on Prayer* (New York, NY: Fleming H. Revell Company, 1904), p. 120.
2. John Wimber, "Prayer: Intimacy with God," *Equipping the Saints*, November-December 1987, p. 3.
3. John Bisagno, *The Power of Positive Praying* (Grand Rapids, MI: Zondervan Publishing House, 1965), p. 71.
4. Timothy K. Jones, "Hands Up in the Hoosier Dome," *Christianity Today*, September 24, 1990, p. 23.
5. Ibid.
6. Francis Frangipane, *The House of the Lord* (Lake Mary, FL: Creation House, 1991), p. 147.
7. Larry Lea, *The Weapons of Your Warfare* (Altamonte Springs, FL: Creation House, 1989), p. 93.
8. Walter Wink, *Naming the Powers* (Philadelphia, PA: Fortress Press, 1984), p. 86.
9. Clinton E. Arnold, *Ephesians: Power and Magic* (Cambridge, England: Cambridge University Press, 1989), pp. 119, 120.

Remitting the Sins of Nations

CHAPTER SEVEN

FRANCIS FRANGIPANE RAISES A CRUCIAL ISSUE WHEN HE observes, "Many saints wonder whether Christians have the authority to pray against the principalities and powers." I am sure some of you reading this book are doing so with that very question in your mind. It is certainly a legitimate question and a necessary starting point.

I agree with Frangipane's response: "The scriptural position is not only that we have authority to war against these powers of darkness, but we have the responsibility to do so as well!" He also uses a play on words that may stick in our minds: "If we do not pray against our spiritual enemies, they will, indeed, prey upon us."[1]

LINCOLN'S EMANCIPATION PROCLAMATION

Many raise questions about the appropriateness of taking the spiritual offensive against principalities and powers because of the Bible's teaching that they have already been defeated. We are told that on the cross Jesus "disarmed principalities and powers [and] made a public spectacle of them" (see Col. 2:15). If they have been defeated, who are we to think that we can add to Jesus' work on the cross?

Nothing, of course, can be added to the blood of Jesus shed on the cross. His sacrifice was made once and for all. Satan has been defeated. Jesus has overcome the world. The outcome of the war is no longer in doubt. But meanwhile we are engaged in mop-up operations. The Kingdom of God is here and we are a part of it, but it will not arrive in its fullness until Jesus' second coming. Then, and only then, will Satan be cast into a bottomless pit and finally into the lake of fire. Until then he is the prince of the power of the air, although a defeated prince who is constantly being pushed back as the gospel spreads throughout the world.

In order to understand this, let's think of Abraham Lincoln's Emancipation Proclamation, which went into effect on January 1, 1863, about 130 years ago. From 1863 on, black Americans have been free and have been granted full citizenship and social equality with all other Americans. No one questions the legality of the Emancipation Proclamation. All the authority of the federal government of the United States of America stands behind it.

Virtually all Americans, however, recognize and are embarrassed that today Afro-Americans as a social unit do not actually enjoy full social equality alongside other Americans. It has taken time to implement in practice what was done legally once and for all by President Lincoln's signature. For many years life did not change at all for multitudes of blacks on southern plantations. It took almost 100 years for some states as a whole to get rid of Jim Crow laws, which prevented blacks from voting, kept them out of certain restaurants and sat them at the back of busses.

It required the burning of urban ghettos in the 1960s to force America to begin to realize that the Emancipation Proclamation needed to be implemented yet more thoroughly. Civil rights leaders and social planners alike are realistic enough to know that only through strenuous and conscientious effort on the part of all Americans will our social situation ever be brought in line with the full legal intent of the Emancipation Proclamation. How long that will take is anyone's guess.

Meanwhile, I myself want to be counted among those Americans who are striving right now to see complete equality and social justice for African-Americans as well as for all other minority groups. The war for liberation was won in 1863, but I also want to be part of winning the mop-up battles for civil rights in the 1990s.

Jesus' death on the cross was the emancipation proclamation for the human race. However, 2,000 years later multitudes are not yet saved and huge segments of the world's peoples live in social disaster areas. Just as I want to see victims of social injustice in our nation receive their rightful freedom, so I also want to see victims of satanic oppression around the world freed from Satan's evil grasp.

In order to do either, however, it is not enough to look back to legitimate legal transactions made 130 or 2,000 years ago. Evil is too great and too aggressive. Tom White of Frontline Ministries says, "Too often the church is *re-active* in responding to this flood. But the role of the redeemed is to be courageously *pro-active* in devising and implementing strategies that penetrate and weaken the influence of evil."[2]

SATAN'S LUST FOR THE NATIONS

One of the things God used to impress Cindy Jacobs to establish her ministry, Generals of Intercession, was the realization that Christians desperately need a strategy. She says, "It became clear that the enemy has a strategy for every nation and ministry."[3]

Scriptures are quite clear that Satan has a lust for power over nations. In Revelation 20 we read that Satan will one day be bound for 1,000 years. The text mentions only one thing this binding will change: "He should deceive the *nations* no

---

We know from the Old Testament that nations can be guilty of corporate sins. This was not only true of Gentile nations, but of Israel as well.

---

more till the thousand years were finished" (Rev. 20:3). When the 1,000 years are over, Satan will be released and the only thing mentioned that he will then do is "go out to deceive the *nations* which are in the four corners of the earth" (Rev. 20:8, italics mine).

I have previously mentioned the harlot who controls peoples, multitudes, *nations* and tongues (see Rev. 17:15). When the evil city of Babylon is thrown down, one of the great cries of rejoicing is that no longer by her sorceries would all the *nations* be deceived (see Rev. 18:23).

The reason I say Satan "lusts" for this power over nations is that more than once we are told that the evil spirit called the harlot commits fornication with political rulers who have authority over nations (see Rev. 17:2; 18:3). Even if the fornication is to be understood figuratively, it connotes nothing less than lust.

These nations Satan desires to control are the same kingdoms he offered to Jesus at the temptation in the wilderness.

And they are the same nations to which Jesus refers in the Great Commission: "Go therefore and make disciples of all the nations" (Matt. 28:19). Jesus commands us to move out in His authority to retake the nations Satan has under his dominion. No wonder we find ourselves in spiritual warfare when we seriously engage in world evangelization. We are threatening Satan at a very sensitive and emotional point. We are taking from him his lovers!

RECOGNIZING THE ENEMY'S STRONGHOLDS

How does Satan, or the territorial spirits he assigns to nations, achieve control? Gwen Shaw, who has long been recognized as a leading strategic-level intercessor, says, "The ruling spirits have no authority to move into an area without permission. Certain conditions give them authority to set up the base of their kingdom from whence they rule over the people in that area."[4] These conditions are frequently referred to as "strongholds." George Otis, Jr., describes strongholds as "nothing less than satanic command and control centers."[5]

Cindy Jacobs argues that the "legal entrances which have allowed Satan to establish the strongholds in the first place" can be seen as the "gates of the city." She points out that in biblical times city gates were "symbols of authority," places where the elders sat to discuss the welfare of the city.[6]

Those who are active in ministries of ground-level spiritual warfare know that frequently demons find entrance points into individuals through trauma, sexual abuse, abortion, curses, substance addiction, the occult or any number of other footholds. In many such cases, inner healing is necessary for effective deliverance. Charles Kraft says that many people give Satan grounds by "hanging onto such emotions as bitterness, unforgiveness, desire for revenge, fear, and the like." He goes on to add, "I believe that there is no problem that a person has with an evil spirit that is not tied to some inner problem."[7] I have heard Kraft say several times that demons are like rats that feed on garbage. Remove the garbage and the rats are relatively easy to kick out!

A similar phenomenon frequently prevails in strategic-level spiritual warfare. Nations as a whole can harbor "garbage" that needs to be cleaned up before principalities and powers can be weakened. It is quite possible, for example, that the shameful way early American settlers treated many American Indians has provided a number of significant historical strongholds for the demonic forces presently at work attempting to tear American society apart. This may be one of the reasons why demonic activity is commonly found to be especially powerful in and around some Indian burial grounds.

Gwen Shaw lists 14 such national or city strongholds that have turned up with some regularity in her years of ministry on strategic-level intercession. They include idolatry; pagan temples; shedding of innocent blood such as through murder, abortion or war; witchcraft; mind control; removal of prayer from schools; sexual perversion; substance abuse; fighting and hatred; occult objects; questionable toys; perverted media; relationships and uncontrolled emotions.[8] The list could be extended almost ad infinitum, but this suffices as a representative sample of national strongholds that may need to be dealt with before certain territorial spirits can be conquered.

REMITTING THE SINS

Suppose demonic strongholds actually exist in a nation or a city, affecting society in general and resistance to the gospel in particular. What can be done about it?

Just as in the case of demonized individuals, if sin is present, repentance is called for, if curses are in effect they need to be broken, and if emotional scars are causing pain, inner healing is needed.

We know from the Old Testament that nations can be guilty of corporate sins. This was not only true of Gentile nations, but of Israel as well. Both Nehemiah and Daniel give us examples of godly persons who felt the burden for the sins of their nations.

Hearing that Jerusalem's wall was broken down and its gates consumed with fire, Nehemiah wept, fasted and prayed. He confessed the sins of the children of Israel in general, seeking to remit the sins of the entire nation. He said, "Both my father's house and I have sinned" (Neh. 1:6). Here is an example of one person, under an anointing of God, meaningfully confessing the sins of an entire nation. This is a component of strategic-level spiritual warfare. His prayers obviously had some effect, and God opened doors that only His power could open for the walls and the city to be rebuilt.

Daniel, through reading Scripture, came to realize that Israel's 70 years of captivity were coming to an end. So he went before the Lord in "prayer and supplications, with fasting, sackcloth, and ashes" (Dan. 9:3). He confessed the sins of his people in detail saying, "Yes, all Israel has transgressed Your law, and has departed so as not to obey Your voice" (Dan. 9:11). Later he said he had confessed "my sin and the sin of my people" (Dan. 9:20).

It is important to note that both Nehemiah and Daniel, while they were standing before God on behalf of their entire nation, confessed not only the corporate sins of their people, but also their individual sins. Those who remit the sins of nations must not fail to identify personally with the sins that were or are being committed even though they might not personally be as guilty of them as some other sins.

ARGENTINA AND AUSTRALIA

In his book *Taking Our Cities for God*, John Dawson gives some specific examples of remitting the sins of nations. In Córdoba, Argentina, in 1978, for example, Dawson and some fellow Youth With a Mission workers were frustrated at the indifference of the people to their message. Through prayer and fasting they discerned that one of the principalities ruling the city was pride. So they confessed their own pride and humbled themselves by kneeling to pray on the sidewalks of some of Córdoba's busy downtown areas. With that a harvest of souls began! Dawson says, "The people were so receptive that they would wait patiently in line for us personally to autograph our gospel tracts."[9]

Dawson also tells of attending a prayer meeting of some 15,000 in Sydney, Australia, in 1979. He speaks of the social psychology of Australia as frequently characterized by a sense of rejection and injustice. Then he tells of a spiritual release that came over the people there "when one leader led the crowd to extend forgiveness toward Britain for the injustice suffered by their forefathers in the establishment of Australia as a penal settlement."[10] This is a case of remitting the sins of a nation, and Dawson is able to report great blessing coming to the churches of Australia subsequent to the event.

But once again in remitting the sins of nations, Dawson agrees with Nehemiah and Daniel, that "we must identify with the sins of the city." He says, "You may be a righteous person who is not involved in any direct way with the vices present in your city." But he feels we must move beyond that. "We can all identify with the roots of any given sin."[11]

THE CHALLENGE OF JAPAN

I never really understood what Nehemiah and Daniel did until

I went to Japan in the summer of 1990. I have been visiting Japan quite frequently in recent years because I have felt God giving me a special burden for Japan, along with Argentina, as a nation where He wants both to use me and teach me in these days.

Several of my visits to Japan have been with Paul Yonggi Cho, for I have joined him in his vision for 10 million Japanese Christians by the year 2000. Frankly, I am somewhat surprised at myself for putting such a goal in print. I always teach my students in church growth classes that setting goals is important, but setting unrealistic goals is a serious mistake. In the natural, nothing is realistic about expecting 10 million Japanese Christians by the year 2000 when our base in 1991 is only 1 million at the most, and probably only one third of them truly committed Christians. Paul Yonggi Cho has more committed Christians in his local congregation in Seoul, Korea, than can be found in the whole nation of Japan!

Although there is little or no hope for this in the natural, in the spiritual I have sincere faith that it will be a reality. I do not know the details of how God will bring this to pass, but I am as sure as I can be that the essence will be some kind of a spiritual battle; strategic-level spiritual warfare that will dramatically increase the receptivity of the Japanese people to the gospel. Political scientists were surprised and even baffled by the rapid collapse of the Iron Curtain. I believe something equally dramatic and equally swift can happen to the spiritual atmosphere of Japan. If it does, the projected 10 million can come into the Kingdom in a relatively short period of time. A large number of Japanese, three out of four, say that if they ever had to choose a religion they would choose Christianity.

The Demonization of a Nation

As I was planning to go to Tokyo in the summer of 1990, I became deeply disturbed by the plans being laid for the new

Emperor Akihito to go through with the *Daijosai* ceremony November 22-23. This ancient Shinto ritual, in a word, openly invites the demonization of an entire nation. In it, the new emperor eats ceremonial rice chosen for him through witchcraft and keeps a personal rendezvous with the highest territorial spirit over the nation, the Sun Goddess, *Amaterasu Omikami.* On a special straw throne, called by some a "god bed," he reportedly engages in either literal or symbolic sexual intercourse with the Sun Goddess. Through this they become one flesh, and traditionally the emperor is then regarded as a god and becomes an object of worship. As the human embodiment of the Japanese people as a whole, the emperor performs this occultic ritual on behalf of the entire nation.

When I went to Japan in August, a few months previous to the *Daijosai,* I, along with many others, called for fervent prayer and fasting that the emperor would exercise his prerogative of *not* going through with the occult ceremony. I, of course, did not know then that my worst fears would be realized and that it would actually happen as planned in November.

Two days before I left for Japan, I spoke to a group at the great Congress on the Holy Spirit and World Evangelization in the Indianapolis Hoosier Dome. I challenged the people to pray for the 10 million Christians in Japan over the next few years and to pray against the evil spiritual activity associated with the projected *Daijosai* ceremony. When I finished, the leader of the meeting invited Cindy Jacobs to come forward and to pray for me and for Japan.

A Prophetic Prayer

Cindy prayed a prophetic prayer, which I am going to record in its entirety:

> *Lord, I thank you that you are sending Peter Wagner to Japan. Father, it was the American people who caused*

great devastation when they dropped the bombs on Hiroshima and Nagasaki. Lord, I thank you that you are sending back an American to undo the atrocity of Hiroshima and Nagasaki. Father, Peter will be used like a nuclear bomb in the Spirit to break apart the darkness that Satan has worked against the nation of Japan and the Japanese people.

Lord, I am asking that you heal the Japanese people of the trauma done during the aftermath of Hiroshima and Nagasaki. Father, you want to use the Japanese people mightily to send missionaries all over the world in this end-time move of your Spirit. Lord, you restore the years the cankerworm and the locust have eaten up in the land of the rising sun and "I the Sun of Righteousness will arise with healing in my wings for the land that I love."

Now, Lord, let your anointing be mighty upon Peter as he brings forth your word to unify and bring restoration to your body, in the name of Jesus. Amen

At the moment I did not regard the prayer as anything out of the ordinary. I left my wife, Doris, who was a member of the 24-hour intercession team for the congress, in Indianapolis and came home to teach my Sunday School class and leave Sunday afternoon for Japan.

While preparing for my class early Sunday morning a strange thing happened. As I was praying about my forthcoming trip to Japan, for the first time I can ever remember doing so, I began to weep openly for a nation. First I got one Kleenex, then I had to get the whole box and put it on my desk. When I calmed down, the telephone rang. It was Doris calling from Indianapolis saying she and others had been praying for Japan. They sensed that the Lord wanted me to repent of the sin of dropping the atomic bomb on Hiroshima and Nagasaki. Such a thought had never before entered my mind.

I was willing to obey God if that was what He wished, so I began reading Nehemiah, sensing that I should share this with the Japanese people. I clearly saw how my father's house

---

We must personally identify with the sins of a given city or nation if God is to use us in remitting those sins.

---

had sinned by dropping the atomic bombs. Even admitting that Truman's decision was wise military strategy, Americans still carried the responsibility of shedding the blood of thousands of innocent Japanese civilians. I felt that I could honestly confess this.

"I Have Sinned"

My problem came with Nehemiah's statement that not only "my father's house" but also "*I have sinned*" (Neh. 1:6, italics mine). My first thought was that I was only a boy of 15 the day the war ended (in fact, VJ Day August 15, 1945, was my 15th birthday). I didn't fight in the war, manufacture a bomb, shoot a gun or kill any Japanese. Then I felt the Holy Spirit come over me strongly and deeply convict me of two things. First, He reminded me that I hated the Japanese people with a sinful hate.

Secondly, God showed me that in Hiroshima and Nagasaki were other 15-year-old boys, as innocent as I was, who never shot a gun or dropped a bomb who are now dead or permanently disabled because of the atomic bomb! The weeping for Japan started again with twice the intensity as before. To this day I can never share that story without losing emotional control.

At that moment I learned what John Dawson meant when he said we must personally identify with the sins of a given city or nation if God is to use us in remitting those sins. I learned why it was that Nehemiah "sat down and wept, and mourned for many days" (Neh. 1:4).

It just so happened that the place where I was staying in Tokyo, the Imperial Hotel, was the building General MacArthur had used for his headquarters while in Japan. It is right across from the grounds of the Imperial Palace, and the auditorium where I was teaching some 1,000 Japanese Christians was adjacent to the palace grounds. After teaching a session or two, I asked my interpreter if he would help me locate some Christians in the audience who had suffered themselves or lost loved ones in Hiroshima and Nagasaki. I wanted them to represent the Japanese people to whom I would confess.

Victims of the Atomic Bomb

We found two representatives from Hiroshima. The first was a man assigned to the military telegraph office in Hiroshima, who had been exposed to radioactivity and also had to give first aid to the wounded and remove several corpses. The second was a woman whose mother-in-law was not physically wounded but who still suffers the psychological effects.

We found two representatives from Nagasaki. The first was a man whose wife and sister-in-law were both exposed to radioactivity, and the sister-in-law died. The other was a woman whose mother went to Nagasaki to help as a nurse, was burned on her arms, and received secondary radioactivity from which she finally recovered.

After an extensive teaching on strategic-level spiritual warfare and remitting the sins of nations with specific application to the evangelization of Japan and the vision for 10 million Japanese Christians by the year 2000, I invited the four to stand by me on the platform. I explained in detail what I was doing, then knelt in humility before the congregation and the four on the platform and begged their forgiveness for my sins and the sins of my fathers. I wept tears of repentance, and when I looked up, handkerchiefs were out all over the auditorium. God was doing a powerful, corporate work. As Pastor Hiroshi Yoshiyama later wrote, "The congregation melted in tears and repentance. We have never had a conference like this before."

I said, "I used to hate the Japanese people, now I love them dearly." With an apology for not knowing how to do the proper Japanese bowing on the occasion, I proceeded to give each an American hug.

The Japanese leader who was serving as master of ceremonies then led the congregation in a spontaneous and powerful session of individual and corporate repentance on the part of the Japanese. They forgave the Americans and then begged forgiveness themselves for what they said were worse sins than the Americans had ever committed. Paul Yonggi Cho, who as a Korean has his own set of feelings about the Japanese, gave me an American hug and said that he also broke down and cried under the power of the Holy Spirit, feeling that important spiritual victories were won that day.

Needless to say, this was a spiritual experience I will never forget.

What Really Happened?

To this day I feel humbled that God would choose to use me as an instrument for remitting the sins of a nation. But what really happened? What difference did it make?

For one thing, I do not believe Japanese-American political relationships crossed some kind of a threshold that day. I think that for this to ever happen the participants will have to be those who have national authority, not a simple seminary professor. Certainly more was done politically some weeks later when U.S. Attorney General Dick Thornburgh knelt in humility before

Mamuro Eto, a 107-year-old Japanese-American minister, in Washington, D.C., and in an official ceremony apologized for America's actions toward Japanese-Americans during World War II. He presented checks of $20,000 to each of 9 elderly Japanese at the ceremony, and said the 65,000 others would soon receive similar redress payments. President Bush wrote, "We can never fully right the wrongs of the past, but we can take a clear stand for justice and recognize that serious injustices were done to Japanese-Americans during World War II."[12]

By mentioning this, I am not implying there was any cause-and-effect relationship between what we did in Tokyo and what happened in Washington. But I do think that in Tokyo something happened in the heavenlies. To what degree I do not know, but I feel sure the territorial spirits over Japan received a significant setback. The *Los Angeles Times* reports that in 1991 Japan commemorated the end of World War II "amid a rare flowering of contrition for its aggression in the war."[13] Much more repentance, confession, forgiveness and humility will be needed before we see the radical changes in Japanese receptivity to the gospel we are praying for.

Changes are not easy to measure. As we gain experience in warfare prayer we will hopefully learn to be more effective. One of the things we need to recognize is the concept of the spiritual relationship between the visible and the invisible.

THE VISIBLE AND THE INVISIBLE

John Dawson says we do well to ask God to help us discern the invisible spiritual forces that are behind the visible problems in the city. He says Christians tend to "read reports of gang violence, corrupt government and child abuse, without clearly establishing the connection to the very real conflict in the unseen realm." Dawson goes on, "I am committed to political and social action, but I realize that electing good people to office is not half as important as gaining victory over principalities and powers."[14]

A key biblical passage for understanding this is the teaching on general revelation in Romans 1. There we are told that God's "invisible attributes are clearly seen, being understood by the things that are made" (Rom. 1:20). One of the purposes of creation is to show forth the glory of the Creator. However, Satan and the forces of evil have corrupted this. They "changed the glory of the incorruptible God into an image made like corruptible man—and birds and four-footed beasts and creeping things" (Rom. 1:23). As a result many created things now glorify Satan rather than God. And people "worshiped and served the creature rather than the Creator" (Rom. 1:25).

This is exactly what has happened in Japan. God created the sun to reflect His eternal glory and majesty. The territorial spirits over Japan have perverted the sun. Japan has come to be known as the "land of the rising sun." The one object on the Japanese flag is the sun. And yet the one who is exalted in that land is not the eternal God who created the sun, but a creature, *Amaterasu Omikami*, the Sun Goddess. Japanese Christian leaders are praying that this will be reversed and that the sun on the Japanese flag will represent the eternal God rather than an evil principality. They believe that prophetically Isaiah 59:19 applies to Japan: "So shall they fear the name of the Lord from the west, and His glory *from the rising of the sun.*" (Italics mine.)

If we are to understand the spiritual dynamic of remitting the sins of nations and cities, it is essential "we do not look at the things which are seen, but at the things which are not seen," as the apostle Paul says. "For the things which are seen are temporary, but the things which are not seen are eternal" (2 Cor. 4:18).

Learning to see the eternal and the invisible is an important part of effective warfare prayer.

■ REFLECTION QUESTIONS ■

1. List some of the sins that the United States has committed against other nations. Then list some that other nations have committed against the United States.
2. One of the most oppressed segments of the American population has been the American Indians. Discuss the concept of remitting sins of nations and what it might do to spiritual powers over those people.
3. If Jesus' death on the cross defeated Satan, why does he have so much power these days?
4. Suppose you identify sins of a nation or a city that need to be remitted. How would you know where or when to do this?
5. Give some examples of how people you know or have heard of "worship and serve the creature rather than the Creator."

Notes
1. Francis Frangipane, *The House of the Lord* (Lake Mary: FL: Creation House, 1991), p. 153.
2. Thomas B. White, *The Believer's Guide to Spiritual Warfare* (Ann Arbor, MI: Servant Publications, 1990), p. 15.
3. Cindy Jacobs, *Possessing the Gates of the Enemy* (Tarrytown, NY: Chosen Books, 1991), p. 32.
4. Gwen Shaw, *Redeeming the Land* (Engeltal Press, P.O. Box 447, Jasper, Arkansas 72641, 1987), p. 81.
5. George Otis, Jr., *The Last of the Giants* (Tarrytown, NY: Chosen Books, 1991), p. 93.
6. Jacobs, *Possessing the Gates*, pp. 235-236.
7. Charles Kraft, *Christianity with Power* (Ann Arbor, MI: Servant Publications, 1989), p. 129.
8. Shaw, *Redeeming the Land*, pp. 81-104.
9. John Dawson, *Taking Our Cities for God* (Lake Mary, FL: Creation House, 1989), p. 20.
10. Ibid., p. 80.
11. Ibid., p. 185.
12. Ronald J. Ostrow, "First 9 Japanese WWII Internees Get Reparations," *Los Angeles Times*, October 10, 1990, p. 1.
13. *Los Angeles Times*, August 13, 1991, "World Report," p. 1.
14. Dawson, *Taking Our Cities for God*, p. 136.

Naming and Mapping the Powers

CHAPTER EIGHT

A S I WRITE THIS BOOK, THE WORLD AGONIZES OVER ONE of the worst natural disasters of recent times. In May of 1991, Bangladesh was ravished by a horrendous cyclone that left around 200,000 dead and millions injured, sick, impoverished, homeless and hopeless.

According to a report in *Time* magazine, of the 10 deadliest storms in the twentieth century, 7 of them have struck Bangladesh. Meteorologists have no consensus why 70 percent of the world's most devastating storms should be in one specific area. But the famous Bengali poet, Rabindranath Tagore, offered a hypothesis 100 years ago. He attributed the phenomenon to Rudra, the Indian storm god.[1]

WHAT IS IN A NAME?

In this chapter I want to look at the names of spiritual

beings in general and territorial spirits in particular. Consider the following scenarios:

Calcutta, India. Robert Linthicum is a pastor, a scholar, a relief and development consultant with World Vision and the author of *City of God; City of Satan,* which is an outstanding biblical theology of the urban church. He arrives in Calcutta for the first time and is almost overwhelmed by a dark, permeating, ominous impression of evil. A frequent traveler to many of the world's urban areas, he senses this is different. Here is the urban world's worst poverty, "a city of suffering, disease, and impoverishment beyond any words to describe adequately."

Throughout the week, a common sight is young men festively parading through the streets to loud music, beating drums and exploding firecrackers. These young men are participating in the annual festival to the Hindu goddess Kali who controls the city. The name Calcutta is derived from the name of the spirit. Linthicum says, "These young men had just left the temple of Kali, in which they had pledged their very souls to the goddess." They hoped to receive in return material goods that might break their vicious cycle of poverty.

"Who is Kali who gathers the souls of young men?" asks Robert Linthicum. "She is the goddess of darkness, evil and destruction in the Hindu pantheon. This is the goddess to whom the entire city is dedicated."[2]

Anaheim, California. Larry Lea, recognized as a top-ranking leader of the current prayer movement, arrives in Anaheim to conduct the first of what has become a long series of "Prayer Breakthroughs." His stated purpose is to "do some serious damage to the strongholds of this city."[3]

Before going to Anaheim, Larry Lea sought the face of God. Among other things, he asked the Lord to show him the identity of the strongholds over that part of Southern California so that his prayers could be more specific. Through prayer he discerned that there were four principal warring spirits over the greater Los Angeles area: spirits of religion, witchcraft, violence and greed. He proceeded to lead the 7,500 believers who attended the massive prayer meeting in the Anaheim Convention Center in warfare prayer against those specific spirits.

Manaos, Brazil. Kjell Sjöberg, a former Swedish missionary to Pakistan and church planter in Sweden, now travels extensively internationally with prayer teams for the specific purpose of strategic-level intercession. He arrives in Manaos, the capital of the state of Amazonas in Brazil, and is teaching believers how to remit the sins of nations. He learns that Amazonas is in a serious environmental crisis because of the wholesale exploitation and destruction of the vast rain forest that is so important to the ecology of the area.

As he and other believers prayed that God would reveal to them the strongholds over the area, they visited the famous luxurious Opera House, built by the rubber barons. A huge mural on the stage of the Opera House shows a woman in a river. It turned out to be a representation of the territorial spirit, Iara, the mother of the rivers who ruled the area long before Columbus discovered America. The Opera House had been built as a temple to the goddess Iara.

When Sjöberg exposed Iara as the chief principality over the region, the host pastor said, "Before I became a Christian I was a worshipper of Iara." They prayed together that the power of Iara would be broken and that the rain forest of Amazonas would be healed.[4]

Do Spirits Really Have Names?
What do we say when we hear that Christian leaders feel they have actually identified territorial spirits *by name*? What goes through our minds when we hear of Rudra or Iara or the spirit of greed or the spirit of violence? It may seem strange to us until we recall that some of them are named just as specifically in the Bible.

Jesus Himself asked for and learned the name of a very powerful spirit called Legion (see Luke 8:30). Some say that was only a numerical description, but whatever it was it came as a direct answer to Jesus' question: "What is your name?" Diana (Artemis) of the Ephesians is specifically named (see Acts 19:23-41). In Philippi, a slave girl had been demonized with a spirit of divination, in the Greek a "python spirit" (see Acts 16:16). Of course, we know the name of the chief evil spirit of all, Satan. Beelzebub (see Luke 11:15), the "lord of the flies," is so high ranking that some equate him with the devil. In Revelation we read of names such as Death (Rev. 6:8), Hades (Rev. 6:8), Wormwood (Rev. 8:11), Abaddon or Apollyon (Rev. 9:11), the harlot (Rev. 17:1), the beast (Rev. 13:1), the false prophet (Rev. 19:20) and others.

In the Old Testament, names of spirits such as Baal (2 Kings 21:3), Ashtoreth (1 Kings 11:5) and Milcom (1 Kings 11:5) are common enough. Some of them have spiritual relatives, so to speak, such as Baal Gad, lord of good fortune (Josh. 11:17), Baal-Berith, lord of the covenant (Judg. 8:33) or Baalath Beer, mistress of the well (Josh. 19:8).

Apart from the Bible, other names of spirits have become known. How accurate they are is anyone's guess, but those who have some expertise in the fields of demonology and angelology seem to have a certain level of consensus on certain names. For example, in the apocryphal book of Tobit, the spirit Asmodeus is prominent and is referred to as the "worst of demons" (Tobit 3:8).

Markus Barth tells us, "Jewish apocalyptic and sectarian writings describe the demons Mastema, Azazel, Sammael, or the arch-enemy Beliar (or Belial) by corresponding attributes."[5] In his *Dictionary of Angels, Including the Fallen Angels*, Gustav Davidson lists hundreds of the names of evil spirits that have turned up since ancient times.[6] Another such source is Manfred Lurker's *Dictionary of Gods and Goddesses, Devils and Demons.*[7]

I am not listing these names and sources in order to glorify evil spirits, but to expose them and make them more vulnerable to attack. At this point I simply want to argue that many spirits really do have names. Not only have they been known throughout history, but anthropologists and missiologists who live among certain people groups of the world today discover that principalities and powers are currently known by name.

Few visitors to Hawaii, for example, have not been informed that the principality over the Big Island is the volcano goddess, Pele. Vernon Sterk says that the Tzotzils, among whom he works in southern Mexico "are very aware of the names of many of the territorial spirits that inhabit their tribal area and villages. They are even able to name some of those which occupy homes and streams."[8] In Bolivia, where I worked for years, the awesome spiritual power of Inti, the sun god, and Pachamama, mother earth, went unchallenged by the majority of the population. It is common knowledge that some Australian Aborigines "can sense the spirits of the land: sometimes smell, sometimes hear and sometimes see them."[9] They know their names only too well.

Calling Spirits by Name
Recognizing that evil spirits do have names raises further questions. How important is it to know these names? If we do know the names, should we use them in warfare prayer?

First, it is helpful to distinguish between proper names and functional names. Kali, Iara, Wormwood, Artemis and Pele are examples of proper names. A spirit of violence, the false prophet or a spirit of witchcraft are functional names, emphasizing what they do. John Dawson, for example, associates a spirit of mammon with New York, violence with Chicago, and political intrigue with Miami. He says, "Getting the exact name of demons at any level is not necessary, but it is important to be aware of the specific nature or type of oppression."[10]

This is confirmed by many who have ministries of deliverance on the ground level. I have observed what appears to be a pattern with friends of mine who have strong ministries of personal deliverance. When they first begin, they often provoke the demons to talk to them and reveal their names and activities. They find that in this overt encounter they can be more sure whether they are gaining the victory and when the demon actually leaves. I believe this is a valid methodology. However, as they grow in skill, experience and spiritual discernment, many of them abandon this methodology and bind the spirits, refusing to allow them to speak, to give their names or to manifest in any way. This quiet form seems to be equally, or in some cases more, effective.

Having said this, we need to recognize that those who deal regularly with the higher levels of the spirit world agree that, while knowing the proper names might not be necessary, it is helpful in many cases. The reason is that there seems to be more power in a name than many of us in our culture might think.

Rumpelstiltskin

Many of us will recall the story of *Rumpelstiltskin*, which we heard as children. This anecdote from German folklore is clearly a tale involving demonic power. The dwarf has access to supernatural power, which allows him to spin flax into gold in order to save the life of the king's bride. Obviously, this supernatural power is not from God because Rumpelstiltskin's price for the service is nothing less than her first child. When the child is born, the poor girl wants to renege, but the dwarf will allow her to do so only on the improbable condition that she guess his name. She discovers his name and the curse is broken. The story has a happy ending, and allows us to see that in the world of the demonic, knowing a proper name can be important.

I am not using a fairy tale to prove a spiritual principle, but only as a well-known illustration of the significance names can have within the worldview of a people (such as pre-Christian Germans) who are under strong demonic oppression. Clinton Arnold affirms that "The calling of names of supernatural 'powers' was fundamental to the practice of magic" in first century Ephesus.[11] Vernon Sterk says that among Tzotzils "The shamans pride themselves in calling on the actual names of all of the different spirits and deities when they have difficult cases."[12]

The *Dictionary of New Testament Theology* summarizes it

Experienced spiritual warriors have found that the more specific we can be in our warfare prayer, the more effective we usually are.

---

well: "In the faith and thought of virtually every nation the name is inextricably bound up with the person, whether of a man, a god or a demon. *Anyone who knows the name of a being can exert power over it*" (emphasis mine).[13]

PUTTING IT INTO PRACTICE

Experienced spiritual warriors have found that the more specific we can be in our warfare prayer, the more effective we usually are. For example, Dean Sherman of Youth With a Mission says, "God will show us the particular influencing spirit so that our prayers can be specific. We can then break these powers in the name of Jesus, and intercede for the Holy Spirit to come and heal the situation." Sherman agrees that "The more specific we are in prayer, the more effective our prayers will be."[14]

Urbanologist Bob Linthicum makes it a point in some of

his urban workshops to have the participants identify the "angel of their city." They must name it, describe it, and discuss how it manifests itself in different aspects of the life of the city, including their churches. He says, "The exercise always proves to be the most stimulating event of the workshop." A feeling grows that the participants are understanding their city in a deeper way. Linthicum's conclusion is: "To be able to name your city's angel and to understand how it is at work both exposes it and enables you to understand the dimensions the church's ministry must undertake if it is truly to confront the principalities and powers!"[15] This has much to do with why the first in Walter Wink's trilogy on principalities and powers is *Naming the Powers*.

Dick Bernal, one of the pioneers of contemporary strategic-level spiritual warfare, says, "I cannot be too emphatic. In dealing with the princes and rulers of the heavenlies, they must be identified."[16] As Larry Lea prays over his church, he often addresses the principalities to the north, south, east and west of his church as persons. He says, for example, "North, you have people God wills to become a part of my church. I command you in the name of Jesus to release every person who is supposed to become a part of this body."[17]

In summary, although it is not always necessary to name the powers, if the names can be found, whether functional names or proper names, it is usually helpful for focusing warfare prayer.

SPIRITUAL MAPPING

A relatively new area of Christian research and ministry closely connected with naming the powers is called "spiritual mapping." Key figures in the development and definition of this field are David Barrett of the Southern Baptist Foreign Mission Board, Luis Bush of the A.D. 2000 Movement and George Otis, Jr., of

The Sentinel Group. David Barrett, who edited the massive *World Christian Encyclopedia*, and who has the most extensive data base for global Christian statistics ever compiled, discerned an area that encompassed North Africa, the Middle East and sections of Asia to Japan. His computer-aided calculations showed that at least 95 percent of the world's unreached peoples and the largest number of non-Christians reside in this area.

The 10/40 Window

Luis Bush observed that this area was situated between the latitudes of 10° and 40° north and drew a rectangle on the map, which he calls "The 10/40 Window." This 10/40 Window is becoming widely accepted by missiologists as the most crucial area for the focus of the forces for world evangelization in the 1990s. Within it are the centers of Buddhism, Confucianism, Hinduism, Islam, Shintoism and Taoism.

George Otis, Jr. says, "By playing host to these religions' nerve centers—and some 95 percent of the world's unreached peoples—the lands and societies of the 10/40 Window can hardly avoid becoming the primary spiritual battleground of the 1990s and beyond. And when the epic conflict finally unfolds, enemy operations will in all likelihood be managed from two powerful strongholds—Iran and Iraq—situated at the epicenter of the Window."[18] Otis points out that strategic-level spiritual warfare seems to be building up at the same geographical location where it started, the Garden of Eden.

This type of discernment enters into spiritual mapping. It is an attempt to see a city or a nation or the world "as it *really is*, not as it *appears to be*."[19] It is based on the assumption that the spiritual reality lies behind the natural. It takes seriously the distinction between the visible and the invisible, as I explained in the last chapter. The apostle Paul says, "We do not look at the things which are seen, but at the things which are not seen" (2 Cor. 4:18).

Otis explains that spiritual mapping "involves superimposing our understanding of forces and events in the spiritual domain on places and circumstances in the material world." The result is a map that is different from any we have yet seen. "On this new map of the world," says Otis, "the three spiritual super-powers we have examined—Hinduism, materialism, Islam—are not entities in themselves. They are, rather, the *means* by which an extensive hierarchy of powerful demonic authorities controls billions of people."[20]

Dean Sherman suggests that one reason we need to do spiritual mapping is that Satan has already done his mapping. "Like any good general, Satan's plans to rule the earth have begun with good maps...Satan knows his battleground." Sherman's experience bears this out. "In Los Angeles," he says, "I have left one suburb for another and felt I had entered spiritually foreign territory." He recommends that we study maps. "Praying geographically will shake up the devil and hinder his plans."[21]

Spiritual Mapping in the Bible

Some will naturally ask whether we have any biblical warrant to do spiritual mapping. A theological underpinning for it revolves around the concept of the visible and the invisible, which I have mentioned (see chapter 7). For specific examples, at least one is given in Scripture.

At one point, God spoke to Ezekiel and said, "You also, son of man, take a clay tablet and lay it before you, and portray on it a city, Jerusalem" (Ezek. 4:1). On a piece of clay, the equivalent of paper in those days, Ezekiel was to draw a map. God then told him to "lay siege against it." This is obviously not a reference to physical warfare, but to spiritual warfare. He was then to take an iron plate and put it between him and the city as if it were a wall, and he was to lay siege against that as well.

Our spiritual maps of the 1990s will not be on clay tablets. They will, no doubt, be generated by computers and printed out on color laser printers. But I believe God wants us to be like Ezekiel and lay siege against the strongholds of the enemy whether they be in cities like Jerusalem, in neighborhoods, unreached people groups or nations as a whole.

Drawing the Maps
Spiritual mapping is such a new endeavor that we do not as yet have seminary courses to train spiritual cartographers or do-it-yourself manuals for beginners. One thing we do know, however, is that accurate spiritual mapping is based on quality historical research. Several of those who have developed some

---

Strategic-level spiritual warfare seems to be building up at the same geographical location where it started, the Garden of Eden.

---

expertise in strategic-level spiritual warfare offer valuable instruction for researchers.

Tom White, for example, says, "Begin research into the ideologies, religious practices, and cultural sins that may invite and perpetuate demonic bondage in your locality. Cities or territories may have distinctive spiritual atmospheres." Discovering the original conditions on which a city was founded is helpful. This can also apply to buildings. White speaks of a Presbyterian Bible College in Taiwan that was having disturbing visitations of evil spirits at night. Research showed that the school had been built on a Buddhist burial ground.[22]

For those who are interested in more details on spiritual research methodology, I recommend books by two of the top leaders in the field, Cindy Jacobs' *Possessing the Gates of the Enemy*[23] and John Dawson's *Taking Our Cities for God*.[24] Cindy

Jacobs provides a list of 7 questions to ask, and John Dawson a list of 20.

Not everything is discovered by research, of course. Discernment of spirits is a spiritual gift that is extremely valuable, for through it spiritual cartographers are given special insights by the Holy Spirit. In many cases they go together: The research triggers questions that lead to prophetic spiritual insights as interpretations of research data. As Tom White says, "Learn to ask questions and listen for the Lord's answers."[25]

Mapping Guadalajara

Not long ago, I visited Guadalajara, Mexico, for the first time. I had been invited to do a church growth conference for around 200 denominational executives from the Mexican Church of God (Cleveland, TN).

When I arrived, I found a city of 6 million people with only 160 evangelical churches. This was appalling because in the 1990s no significant area of Latin America should have been less than 5 percent Protestant. Many have 10 to 20 percent, and neighboring Guatemala has more than 30 percent. With a minimum of 5 percent evangelicals, Guadalajara should have had 1,500 churches, not 160. At the level of Guatemala there would have been 9,000 churches.

What was wrong?

As I pondered this, one of the things that I believe came from the Holy Spirit was the realization that these Mexican pastors were high quality Christian leaders. I imagined a scenario in which these 200 Mexican pastors were on one side of a room, and 200 Guatemalan pastors were on the other side. If I gave them a theology test, both groups would score virtually the same. If I examined them on their morality there would be no significant difference. Likewise a survey of denominational spectrum, evangelistic methodologies or motivation for evangelism. What, then, was the variable? How can we explain explosive church growth on one side of a border and staunch resistance to the gospel on the other side?

It occurred to me that the Mexican pastors were not the perpetrators of this disparity in church growth. They did not need to be kicked, scolded or subjected to another guilt trip. They were victims! Victims of wicked spiritual forces that apparently had been weakened in Guatemala, but remained entrenched in Guadalajara.

As I began talking to the pastors about these concerns I was somewhat surprised to find very little awareness among them of strategic-level spiritual warfare. I wouldn't have been that surprised had they been Baptists or Presbyterians, but they were Pentecostals.

"The Devil's Corner"

I went back to my hotel greatly disturbed and prayed that God would give me discernment. Then I went downstairs to get a cup of coffee, and God answered my prayer sooner than I had expected. I casually picked up a tourist magazine and in it discovered the seat of Satan in Guadalajara. At the center of the city is the Plaza Tapatía, and on the list of tourist attractions in the Plaza Tapatía was a place called "The Devil's Corner" (*el Rincón del Diablo*)!

Curious, I asked the pastor who was acting as my chauffeur to take me to the Plaza Tapatía. When we were about three or four blocks away I prayed out loud in the front seat of the car for protection. I could see that my friend was somewhat surprised at this. We parked and walked through the plaza to the Devil's Corner. I felt chills up and down my spine when I saw what was there. Beautifully engraved in the marble sidewalk was a compass pointing to the north, the south, the east and the west! Through it, Satan had symbolically claimed total control of the city!

On our way back to the conference my friend said, "That

was a strange experience for me. I have been to the Plaza Tapatía a hundred times, and I never felt the blanket of spiritual oppression over me that I felt this time."

I responded, "Don't be surprised. The first hundred times you went as a tourist. The principalities have no problem with tourists entering their territory. But this time you went as an invading enemy and apparently the forces of evil knew this and responded accordingly." He then told me he understood why I had prayed for protection.

In my next session, I told the group about this experience in elementary spiritual mapping. They responded very warmly, indicating they probably never would have done that themselves since they had not been aware of that kind of approach.

Then Pastor Sixto Jiménez stood up. He was one of the few in the group who actually lived in Guadalajara and he served as the superintendent of the region. Jiménez said that, without knowing much about warfare prayer, a group of 60 pastors from different denominations around the city had begun to gather for prayer once a month about 6 months ago. Then he said, "Last Sunday we had 26 baptisms in our church, the largest number of baptisms in history!" I rejoiced with them that God was already at work in weakening the principalities and powers, which had for so long been blinding the minds of the residents of Guadalajara.

BACK TO ARGENTINA

Throughout this book, I have made frequent references to Argentina as a principal laboratory in which some of us are testing the theories of strategic-level spiritual warfare. One of the keys to the substantial evangelistic results in the city of Resistencia was naming the spirits over that city: Pombero, Curupí, San La Muerte, Reina del Cielo, witchcraft and Freemasonry (see chapter 1). Under the coaching of Cindy Jacobs, the

Argentine pastors prayed strongly and specifically against these principalities.

Three large art panels in the main plaza helped considerably. Cindy said, "These panels are like a map of the spiritual realm. They reveal the plans and intentions of the enemy." She then pointed out how a huge snake represented witchcraft and that it already had several Christian fish in its belly. The fowls of the air represented religious spirits. The bony figure playing the violin was San La Muerte. A cloud-like figure with the sun and moon stood for the Queen of Heaven.[26]

The case of Resistencia shows how naming the powers and spiritual mapping go hand in hand.

The next target for Edgardo Silvoso's Harvest Evangelism is a three-year evangelistic thrust in the city of La Plata, just south of Buenos Aires. A young Argentine pastor with gifts of discernment of spirits, Victor Lorenzo, has been assigned the spiritual mapping of this city of 800,000.

Masonic Symbolism

Victor Lorenzo discovered that La Plata had been founded a little over 100 years ago by Dardo Rocha, a high-ranking Mason. He designed the city according to the dictates of Masonic symbolism and numerology. He installed two diagonal avenues to transect the city, forming a symbolic pyramid. Then he went to Egypt, brought back some mummies and buried them in strategic places to help assure that the city would remain under the demonic control he was helping to manipulate.

The huge Plaza Moreno in front of the central cathedral has four bronze statues of beautiful women, each representing a curse on the city. They had been ordered from a foundry in Paris run by Masons. The only other statue in the plaza is a muscular archer with a drawn bow. The arrow is aimed directly at the cross on top of the cathedral. And the cathedral has no cross! Apparently the evil archer is to be seen as having eliminated Christ crucified (Catholics often use a crucifix instead of an empty cross) from the center of Christianity in the city.

On a straight line, out from the front of the cathedral are the centers of power: the city hall, the provincial capitol, the legislature, the police department, the municipal theater and others. They are on what would have been 52nd Avenue, but there is no street. Instead there is a tunnel under all those buildings where the Masonic rituals have been, and possibly are yet, held.

The number 6 figures prominently in the city layout, and in the architecture of the public buildings the number 666 appears time and again. Grotesque demonic faces, beautifully painted and gilded, form a prominent part of the decor of many of the buildings. Victor Lorenzo has already discovered much more evidence, and God will show him much more as he continues the spiritual mapping of La Plata.

I need to reiterate what I have mentioned frequently—naming the powers and spiritual mapping are not to be seen as ends in themselves, much less as means of glorifying Satan and his evil forces. In the Persian Gulf war, for example, discovering and plotting Saddam Hussein's communications nerve centers was not designed to glorify Saddam Hussein, but to crush him and rob him of his power. Likewise, naming the powers is designed to bind the strongman and weaken his powers over the souls of 800,000 people in La Plata who have yet to receive Jesus Christ as Savior and Lord.

Collectively, we have a long way to go in learning how to name the powers and do spiritual mapping with the excellence that God desires. In this chapter I have simply tried to provide a starting point for others to build on. My conclusion is that naming the powers and mapping them has the potential to furnish a new and important tool that will be used by God for extending His Kingdom throughout the earth in our days.

■ REFLECTION QUESTIONS ■

1. How accurate do you think it might be to attribute phenomena such as cyclones to spiritual forces?
2. In your studies of history or geography have you come across any names that might identify territorial spirits? Talk about them.
3. Could you attempt to identify the "angel of your city"? How would you test or validate your conclusion?
4. Discuss a potential "spiritual map" of your city. What would be some of the more obvious boundaries?
5. Why is it considered a danger to become overly fascinated with who the devil is and what he does?

Notes
1. James Walsh, "Cyclone of Death," *Time*, May 13, 1991, p. 29.
2. Robert C. Linthicum, *City of God; City of Satan* (Grand Rapids, MI: Zondervan Publishing House, 1991), pp. 64-65.
3. Julia Loren, "Lea Leads Prayer Fight," *Charisma & Christian Life*, August 1989, p. 30.
4. Kjell and Lena Sjöberg, *Newsletter*, March 6, 1991, p. 3.
5. Markus Barth, *Ephesians* (Garden City, NY: Doubleday & Company, 1974), p. 803.
6. Gustav Davidson, *A Dictionary of Angels, Including the Fallen Angels* (New York, NY: The Free Press, 1967).
7. Manfred Lurker, *Dictionary of Gods and Goddesses, Devils and Demons* (New York: NY: Routledge & Kegan Paul, 1987).
8. Vernon J. Sterk, "Territorial Spirits and Evangelization in Hostile Environments," *Engaging the Enemy*, C. Peter Wagner, ed. (Ventura, CA: Regal Books, 1991), p. 159.
9. Daniel Batt, "Yiwarrapalya: Highway of Holiness," *On Being*, May 1991, p. 9.
10. John Dawson, *Taking Our Cities for God* (Lake Mary, FL: Creation House, 1989), p. 156.
11. Clinton E. Arnold, *Ephesians: Power and Magic* (Cambridge, England: Cambridge University Press, 1989), p. 54.
12. Sterk, *Engaging the Enemy*, p. 159.
13. H. Bietenhard, "Name," *The New International Dictionary of New Testament Theology, Vol. 2* (Grand Rapids, MI: Zondervan Publishing House, 1976), p. 648.
14. Dean Sherman, *Spiritual Warfare for Every Christian* (Frontline Communications, Box 55787, Seattle, WA 98155, 1990), p. 100.
15. Linthicum, *City of God; City of Satan*, p. 75.

16. Dick Bernal, *Storming Hell's Brazen Gates* (San Jose, CA: Jubilee Christian Center, 1988), p. 57.
17. Larry Lea, *Could You Not Tarry One Hour?* (Altamonte Springs, FL: Creation House, 1987), p. 93.
18. George Otis, Jr., *The Last of the Giants* (Tarrytown, NY: Chosen Books), pp. 98-99.
19. Ibid., p. 85.
20. Ibid., pp. 85-86.
21. Sherman, *Spiritual Warfare*, pp. 93-94.
22. Thomas B. White, *The Believer's Guide to Spiritual Warfare* (Ann Arbor, MI: Servant Publications, 1990), p. 136.
23. Cindy Jacobs, *Possessing the Gates of the Enemy* (Tarrytown, NY: Chosen Books, 1991), pp. 237-238.
24. Dawson, *Taking Our Cities*, p. 85.
25. White, *The Believer's Guide*, p. 137.
26. Jane Rumph, *We Wrestle Not Against Flesh and Blood* (Privately published Argentina report, 1990), p. 67.

The Rules for City Taking

CHAPTER NINE

GROWING CONSENSUS AMONG CHRISTIAN LEADERS IS that the most strategic geographical area for the evangelization of a nation is the city. Two of those who have been clearly bringing this to our attention are John Dawson and Floyd McClung. The titles of their books, *Taking Our Cities for God* and *Seeing the City with the Eyes of God*, respectively, reflect this insight. Dawson sees the cities as the mind and heart of a nation. He says, "A nation is the sum of its cities."[1] McClung says, "Cities are the mountain peaks of society; trends, ideologies and fashions are born in the fermenting cauldron of city life and then flow down and out to influence the populace."[2]

Roger Greenway, an urban missiologist, in a recent review of these two books admits that traditional evangelicals should take note. He says, "Perhaps we have drifted, in practice if not in theory, from the biblical world view that takes a personal devil seriously and defines mission as spiritual warfare against the active forces of darkness."[3]

THINKING STRATEGICALLY

As I have mentioned several times, the ultimate focus of this book is world evangelization. Warfare prayer is not an end in itself, but a means of opening the way for the Kingdom of God to come, not only in evangelism, but also in social justice and material sufficiency.

As we look at the world, it is only natural that our attention is first drawn to nations as target units. That is why I so strongly support James Montgomery's DAWN (Discipling a Whole Nation) Movement, a brilliant strategy to catalyze the Christian forces in each nation to evangelize their country by multiplying churches. A more advanced set of target groups are unreached peoples, and missiologists are discovering within each nation fairly large numbers of diverse people groups, many of whom are virtually untouched by the gospel.

The other unit we need to look at when we develop evangelistic strategy, as I have mentioned, is the city. John Dawson says that if we are serious about discipling nations we must grasp their reality. "That means the gospel must transform the spiritual, philosophical and physical life of a nation's cities." He then gives a challenge, which I echo: "Let's lift up Christ's banner in the dirtiest, darkest places. Let's take on the giant of the impersonal, looming city."[4]

The most sophisticated strategy for evangelizing a city we have at the present time is Edgardo Silvoso's Harvest Evangelism. In chapter 1, I told of Silvoso's first experiment in the city of Resistencia, Argentina. Through effective warfare prayer, the number of evangelical believers in the city doubled over the course of the *Plan Resistencia*. As I write, the city of La Plata is the current focus of a three-year effort, and I look for similar results there.

It may not be long before numerous other cities in Argentina are involved in similar efforts for evangelization, prayer, spiritual warfare and church multiplication in their cities. It has the potential for transforming a nation to a degree rarely seen in Christian outreach ministries of the past.

My wife, Doris, and I have been working very closely with Edgardo Silvoso in these cities, and from this experience, along with many other citywide prayer movements we have been directly or indirectly involved with, some rather clear guidance for this type of warfare ministry are emerging.

I call these *Six Rules for Taking a City*. I suspect there may be more than six rules, but I do not suspect there are less. My best advice is not to leave out any of these six rules if you are serious about making a permanent spiritual impact on your city.

RULE #1: THE AREA
Select a manageable geographical area with discernible spiritual boundaries.

A common tendency for beginners is to select a target area too large for warfare prayer to be very effective. I do not mean there won't be occasions when God will call some to pray for the large-scale things, especially when the prayers are focused on critical issues.

I believe, for example, that God used the prayers of Dick Eastman, Gwen Shaw, Beth Alves and many others I will never hear about to bring down the Berlin Wall and the Iron Curtain. I believe God is using Hector Pardo and Christy Graham to open Albania to the gospel. I believe God used Cathy Schaller to depose Manuel Noriega. I believe God used John Dawson to lower the crime rate in Los Angeles during the 1984 Olympics.

I believe God used my wife, Doris, and Cindy Jacobs to turn around the economy in Argentina and to encourage the Argentine government to return 150,000 hectares of land to the native Indians.

Let me explain. I do not think the prayers of any one of these individuals or the group they prayed with bore a one-to-one cause-and-effect relationship to any of these social changes. But the individuals I named are all personal friends whom God uses powerfully in prayer. I know each one prayed very specifically for the situation described, and each one testified after a particular season of prayer that they sensed something had been changed in the spiritual realm.

The secret behind the effectiveness of these high level warfare pray-ers is simple. *Before* they prayed, these intercessors sought and discerned the will of God, determined the *kairos* or divinely appointed time, and then obeyed God's call to pray according to His will. Each of them knew that any number of other intercessors were also hearing from God and praying the same way. When they sensed they had the victory, it did not mean to any of them that they had single-handedly brought down the enemy forces. But they knew they had a part, even though a small one, in the final outcome. They might not have scored touchdowns, but they might well have made firstdowns.

Manageable Units

Although only a relatively few intercessors may be called upon to participate in such large-scale prayer efforts, God is calling multitudes of intercessors to engage in warfare praying for the cities of the world. Some cities as such are small enough areas to be manageable. I believe my own city of Pasadena, California, is an example. A prayer effort called "Pasadena for Christ" is underway and it very intentionally includes only the city of Pasadena, and a small annex called Altadena. Neighboring cities such as Arcadia, Sierra Madre, South Pasadena and San

Marino are different and will be developing their own prayer strategies.

This, of course, is a form of spiritual mapping that will resurface frequently as we go through the six rules.

I am one of the participants in an exciting gathering of pastors and other Christian leaders in the "Love L.A." prayer meetings led by Jack Hayford of Church On The Way and Lloyd Ogilvie of Hollywood Presbyterian Church. We meet three times a year and have had as many as 1300 and as few as 400 in the meetings. These meetings have had several important benefits. They have built the spiritual morale and faith of hundreds and hundreds of pastors across denominational, racial, sectional, socioeconomic, and church size barriers. Recently, several thousand people from the churches represented gathered for a citywide prayer meeting to pray for revival, unity, and the social problems of Los Angeles.

However, the most important result of these larger meetings, in my opinion, is that they have stimulated the formation of smaller gatherings in areas of the greater Los Angeles basin. The advantages of these regional meetings is that the prayer efforts can be directly focused on the specific needs of each region. At this writing, I have in my hand a list of 13 regional prayer groups in the San Fernando Valley, 12 in the San Gabriel Valley, 5 in San Bernardino County, 3 in the Antelope Valley, 11 in Los Angeles, 7 in the Long Beach area, 5 in Orange County and 7 in the South Bay area. Not that all of these will become effective warfare prayer units for taking their cities, but it is a significant start: Some of them will. Their effectiveness will increase not only as they target specific cities, but also as they discern the smaller units of their city.

Christ for the City
The most sophisticated design I am aware of for praying effectively for the smaller units in the city is the Latin America Mis-

sion's "Christ for the City" program developed by John Huffman. The vision for this ministry came as Huffman was flying over Mexico City when God showed him a picture of huge Indian gods standing behind the mountains over Mexico City, holding down the city. He said, "God, what will I do? What do you want us to do about this?" God answered by giving him the prayer program for Christ for the City.[5]

Christ for the City begins by breaking the city down into neighborhoods, manageable geographical areas. In Medellin,

---

It is important for pastors to understand that the unity required to take a city for Christ is not doctrinal unity, legal unity, political unity or philosophy of ministry unity, but spiritual unity.

Colombia, for example, they have designated 255 neighborhoods in a city of 3 million. Each one of these neighborhoods is mapped in detail, showing each lot, what buildings are on the lot, what color house, and the name of the family or families who live there.

The maps are distributed to prayer groups in the city, in other parts of the country and in other countries. These are groups who have previously committed themselves to do concentrated, specific warfare praying for that neighborhood during a designated period of two weeks. Teams on the site are also praying through the neighborhood itself. If at least three prayer groups report spiritual impressions about a particular household or place, trained workers go right in and solicit specific prayer requests for that house. When the two weeks are over, local team members do a blanket visitation of all the homes in the target neighborhood.

A pilot project was launched in Medellin in 1989. In 1989 the evangelical church grew 44 percent, from 9,000 to 13,000. The following year the evangelical population grew 50 percent, from 13,000 to 18,500. During that same 2-year span, the total number of churches increased from 103 to 140.

Prayer groups outside the city keep touch through fax machines and computer modems. In Medellin, one of the participating prayer groups was a Baptist General Conference church in the United States. Even though they had no tradition of receiving prophetic words from the Lord, one day the group heard clearly that there was something wrong with a certain vacant lot in the neighborhood they were praying for, and they faxed the information to Medellin. A ministry team visited the lot and found five occult objects cursed and buried by witches to control the neighborhood. They were destroyed, and the gospel flowed freely.

On a more personal level, a young man named Fulvio visited a house with nine family members, all staunchly opposed to the gospel. But when Fulvio asked, they said they would permit him to pray for the healing of one of them who was sick, but he shouldn't expect very much to happen. He prayed, the person was healed and came to the Lord. Now all nine people in that home are meeting regularly for Bible study.[6]

Once you know the manageable area God wants you to pray for, it is time to get the leaders together.

RULE #2: THE PASTORS
Secure the unity of the pastors and other Christian leaders in the area and begin to pray together on a regular basis.

There is no substitute for the unity of the pastors of the city as a foundation for effective spiritual warfare. The reason for this is that the pastors are the spiritual gatekeepers of the city. This is not to disparage numbers of gifted lay leaders and full-time Christian workers who are not pastors. But it is to point out that in a given city the highest spiritual authority has been delegated to pastors. If we don't know this, Satan certainly does and he does his best to keep pastors from getting together, especially to pray.

When asked where one starts when attacking the evil influences over a city, Dick Bernal says that it must start with the churches. "Pray that the pastors of your city will unite in an all out effort to rid your city of alien entities."7

It is important for pastors to understand that the unity required to take a city for Christ is not doctrinal unity, legal unity, political unity or philosophy of ministry unity, but spiritual unity. The basis is mutual agreement as to who the real enemy is. Too many pastors have been under the impression that they are each other's enemy. This, I am happy to report, is breaking down rapidly and dramatically across our nation. Our country is in too much of a spiritual and social crisis to allow the bickering to continue. Francis Frangipane says, "Today God is calling us to cease fighting with one another and to become a family that fights for each other."8 I couldn't agree more.

Although it might be ideal to think of one hundred percent of the pastors of an area in spiritual agreement and praying together, in many cases that is unrealistic. If we wait for one hundred percent, we may never get to the battle. It is almost inevitable that certain pastors will be grumpy, indifferent, burned out, hung up on some doctrinal issues or even effectively screened out by the forces of darkness. Still, it is realistic to expect a consensus of a considerable number of influential pastors who will agree to meet together for two hours once a month or so to pray.

Until that happens, it is not wise to proceed much further. Joel says, "Gather the elders...into the house of the Lord your God, and cry out to the Lord" (Joel 1:14).

RULE #3: THE BODY OF CHRIST

Project a clear image that the effort is not an activity simply of Pentecostals and charismatics, but of the whole Body of Christ.

One of Satan's common devices to halt spiritual warfare on any level is to get Christians saying to each other, "Oh, that's something those charismatics do!" The unspoken implication is that those of us who are Christians of "the more respectable stripe" would not think of becoming involved in such "disreputable" activity.

Edgardo Silvoso, a graduate of Multnomah School of the Bible and a member of a non-charismatic Bible church, carries excellent evangelical credentials, and has addressed this issue directly. He says, "Satan's number one scheme is to turn spiritual warfare into a divisive issue. Spiritual warfare is and must remain a Christian issue."[9] Silvoso does spiritual warfare seminars across the country, particularly geared to evangelicals who need encouragement.

Predictably, when a citywide prayer effort is announced that includes strategic-level spiritual warfare, the first ones to jump aboard are usually the charismatics and Pentecostals. If they are not warned against it, they can easily find themselves in control and develop a program of action using a style that sends an unintended message to many evangelical leaders: "We're going to do it our way and if you want to be a part of it, you can join us." If that happens, it can weaken the citywide effort.

The highest level public power encounter I know of in America was in all probability Larry Lea's renowned Prayer Breakthrough in San Francisco on Halloween of 1990. It drew the attention of the mass media to the extent not seen for a

Protestant religious event since Billy Graham's Los Angeles crusade in 1979. In his book, *Curses: What They Are and How to Break Them*, Dick Bernal tells of the dramatic conversion of Eric Pryor, the wicca high priest of the New Earth Temple, who publicly cursed Larry Lea before the event.[10] This in itself is convincing testimony to the power of God that was released during the Breakthrough.

That is why I was disappointed when I read in an Associated Press report: "The event is a function of a Pentecostal-Charismatic movement that sees satanic princes and 'territorial spirits' ruling over particular cities, industries and subcultures."[11] I was disappointed because I knew this is not just the opinion of a secular journalist, but also of many Christian leaders.

As an evangelical, my plea to our Pentecostal brothers and sisters is patience. A growing number of evangelicals across the country are ready to jump on board and join a prayer movement for their cities, but it usually takes them a little more time, especially when something as new as strategic-level spiritual warfare is involved. Evangelicals are trained to ask theological questions and to do as the Bereans did, "searched the Scriptures daily to find out whether these things were so" (Acts 17:11). One of my purposes for this book is to argue that praying for the cities does have biblical and theological integrity. But I fear some evangelicals will write it off with the comment that it proves what they have suspected for years—Peter Wagner is really a charismatic even though he says he is not!

The good news is that the situation is getting better these days, not worse. More and more leaders are being moved powerfully by the Holy Spirit to see themselves not primarily as charismatics, Pentecostals, evangelicals or liberals, but as members of the Body of Christ. This in itself will hasten the weakening of the enemy and the advance of God's Kingdom.

RULE #4: THE SPIRITUAL PREPARATION

Assure the spiritual preparation of participating leaders and other Christians through repentance, humility and holiness.

Violate this rule or take it lightly, and you will end up with many wounded, discouraged and unhappy warriors. I need not elaborate on this in great detail because chapter 6, "Equipping the Warriors," dealt in depth with the spiritual condition of the individuals who participate in praying for a city.

When Edgardo Silvoso began to implement the "La Plata Plan" in Argentina, he found that the spiritual level of the church members in the city was not extremely high. Many of them, as a matter of fact, were demonized to one degree or another. Many had succumbed to temptations of the flesh. They desired to serve God, but they knew they needed some help.

For this reason, Silvoso postponed any public warfare prayer until some inner healing was done. Cindy Jacobs was called upon to do an inner healing seminar, first for the pastors and their spouses and then for the believers in general. When my wife, Doris, who accompanied Cindy on the trip, returned she said that in all her ministry she had never seen an out-pouring of the power of God to this degree. At points in the seminar hundreds and hundreds of people were weeping aloud in repentance. Many confessed their sins. Enemies reconciled and became friends. One crippled woman who was suffering from polio forgave her mother under the power of the Holy Spirit and was instantly healed. Another who had lost her cheekbone in an automobile accident became the center of attention as those around her watched the new cheekbone being formed before their eyes.

The net result is that the faith of the believers is now high, they are praying for each other, they are breaking curses left over from the days when some were in witchcraft, they are casting out demons, and the vessels that God wants to use to take the city are being cleansed. The Body of Christ is more holy than it was before.

Whether they are holy enough for strategic-level warfare or when they will be is not an easy question. One of the signs of this maturity is that believers begin truly *obeying* Christ as well as just *following* Him. God's demand for holiness often separates the sheep from the goats. John Wimber says, "In the 90s look for increased tension between Christians who see Christ as their helper and those who see Him as their Master. I suspect that churches will split over these issues."[12] I wouldn't doubt it at all.

RULE #5: THE RESEARCH

Research the historical background of the city in order to reveal spiritual forces shaping the city.

When I discussed spiritual mapping in the last chapter I mentioned how helpful it was to do research on the city. I will not repeat that, but simply give two illustrations, one from an old city and one from a fairly new city.

Manchester, England. I am in correspondence with Richard C. Lockwood of Manchester who has begun the process of researching his city with spiritual discernment. Spiritual people there agree that they feel a heaviness of spirit in the Manchester area, and this heaviness seems to center on the pre-Roman site on which the Cathedral was constructed. The popular teaching that the name "Manchester" was of Roman origin has proved to be incorrect. It more likely goes back to Celtic times and has a meaning which is connected with a "high place." It will take time to find the information that might provide important clues to the nature of the city.

Lockwood comments that it requires little spiritual discernment to identify the territorial spirits influencing the city today:

rebellion, homosexuality, apathy and lethargy. "However, it is the overriding power behind these that needs revealing before effective prayer can prevail."[13]

Brasilia, Brazil. Let me return to Kjell Sjöberg, whom I introduced in the last chapter. Sjöberg's international prayer ministry recently took him to Brasilia, the capital of the nation, which was designed and constructed in 1960 by President Juscelino Kubitschek. Sjöberg reports that Kubitschek was a spiritist who believed in reincarnation, and who thought he himself was the reincarnation of Pharaoh Akhnaton who lived 3,300 years ago and built a new capital for his nation. Many buildings are shaped like Egyptian pyramids or temples. The buildings housing the centers of power are located in triangles, making a hexagram. The numerology of the Egyptian Tarot and the Hebrew Kabbala is prominent throughout. The shape of the city is that of an Egyptian Ibis bird (although some tourist guides make it out to be in the shape of an airplane).[14]

This kind of information, which reveals spiritual forces present from the time of the designing of the city, becomes extremely useful to the intercessors who participate in the city-wide prayer effort.

RULE #6: THE INTERCESSORS

Work with intercessors especially gifted and called to strategic-level warfare, seeking God's revelation of: (a) the redemptive gift or gifts of the city; (b) Satan's strongholds in the city; (c) territorial spirits assigned to the city; (d) corporate sin past and present that needs to be dealt with; and (e) God's plan of attack and timing.

Some of the key players in a well-developed warfare prayer strategy for a city will be intercessors. If the work is going to be done well, gifted intercessors need to be identified, encouraged and released to stand in the gap.

Every Christian has a role of prayer in general and intercession in particular. But God has chosen some Christians and given them a special gift of intercession. If this sounds strange, just compare it to the role that every Christian has to be a witness, but only a small number have received a spiritual gift of evangelist. The whole body cannot be an eye, only some of the members are supposed to be.

I describe the gift of intercession in my book *Your Spiritual Gifts Can Help Your Church Grow*. I list it as one of the 27 gifts, but I freely admit it is one that has no direct biblical statement as a gift. Although some may disagree with me, I am certain enough such a gift exists from simple observation over the years that I am prepared to define it:

> The gift of intercession is the special ability that God gives to certain members of the Body of Christ to pray for extended periods of time on a regular basis and see frequent and specific answers to their prayers to a degree much greater than that which is expected of the average Christian.[15]

Some rather extensive research I have done on intercessors, and which I will describe in detail in another book in this series, shows that gifted intercessors ordinarily pray from two to five hours a day. Much of their time is spent hearing from God. Intercessors will frequently say to each other in a sort of insider's language: "She's wonderful. She really hears from God." Intercessors tend to rate themselves more on what they hear than on what they say.

Cindy Jacobs characterizes intercessors as those who act as enforcers of God's will on earth. God has chosen that His will be done through our asking and taking dominion. She says, "Through our taking dominion over the works of Satan in the earth and praying in the name of our King, we establish His will on earth as it is in heaven."[16]

Intercessors are found in almost every church, and certainly in every city with a reasonable number of churches. Very few pastors are also intercessors. Therefore both pastors and intercessors are needed to pray effectively for a city. The pastors function largely in an authority role and the intercessors function largely in a prophetic role. They hear from God, and can communicate this to others. They should be formed into a group to harmonize, encourage and hold each other accountable.

Through them and also through the pastors and other lay Christians, those who are praying for the city should seek God's revelation of several things:

A. The Redemptive Gift or Gifts of the City

John Dawson believes each city is intended by God to be a place of personal liberation. He says, "I believe our cities have the mark of God's sovereign purpose on them. Our cities contain what I call a redemptive gift."[17] He argues that it is more important to determine the redemptive gift of the city than to identify the nature of evil principalities, although both are needed.

An example is Omaha, Nebraska. Historically, Omaha was the supply station for wagon trains taking pioneers westward. Christian leaders there see today's Omaha as a center for equipping a new breed of pioneer—those who are taking the gospel out to the unreached people of the world. I agree with John Dawson who comments, "Now that's a vision worth living for."[18]

B. Satan's Strongholds in the City

Historical research and spiritual mapping feed into this activity of the intercessors. Most intercessors called to strategic-level spiritual warfare have the spiritual gift of discernment of spirits. Floyd McClung says, "Exercising the gift of discernment of spirits is crucial. We must know if we are battling demonic powers or dealing just with sin and its consequences in the culture. The two are not always the same."[19]

McClung tells of his amazement on a ministry trip to Norway at the many believers there who were struggling with deep, life-controlling fears. He found that this was a widespread problem in the whole nation. Then he went back and discovered how Christianity had first come to Norway. A king marched through the nation and forced all the citizens to become Christians or face execution. Christianity started with a national bloodbath! McClung comments, "Satan takes advantage of this kind of a national trauma, and seeks to use it to establish spiritual strongholds."[20] Intercessors will pray this kind of information through and seek God's revelation on how it should be dealt with in quite specific ways.

In a target city, principalities and powers may have different strongholds in different sectors of the city or even in different neighborhoods. As we develop our Pasadena for Christ effort here in my city, we are very much aware of differences in the spiritual atmosphere, for example, in Northwest Pasadena as compared to Hastings Ranch, and Linda Vista as compared to East Pasadena. Within Northwest Pasadena itself, residents sense a difference between the King's Manor area against Howard and Navarro where John Perkins has his Harambee Center. We do not yet know the deeper meanings of all this, but we have a team of intercessors led by Lou Engle working on it.

C. Territorial Spirits Assigned to the City

To the degree possible, the intercessors should seek to know the names, either functional or proper, of the principalities assigned to the city as a whole and to various geographical, social or cultural segments of the city. I explained this concept of naming the powers with its limitations and its strengths in the last chapter, so there is no need to elaborate further.

D. Corporate Sin Past and Present
That Needs to Be Dealt With

The story Floyd McClung tells of the Norwegian king who murdered those who would not become Christians is an example of past corporate sin that needs to be dealt with. A good bit of information on this is included in chapter 7, "Remitting the Sins of Nations." There I mentioned Japan.

It is encouraging to know that the Japanese Christian leaders are taking national repentance very seriously. In 1990, two high-level apologies were made to the people of Korea. The Church of Christ in Japan published a resolution confessing Japan's sin and offering an apology to the Korean people. Then Rev. Koji Honda, a revered elder statesperson of Japanese evangelical Christianity, made a detailed confession and apology at the Asia Missions Congress '90 held in Seoul, Korea. Among many other things he said, "Dear brothers and sisters of Asia, please forgive the sins that the Japanese people committed in your countries. I think especially of Korea and once again beg your forgiveness of these repulsive, unpardonable sins [which he already had listed] in the name of our Lord and Redeemer."[21]

American sociologists tell us that two of the most oppressed social cohorts in our nation are African-American males and American Indians. *Time* magazine, in an article analyzing the frightening downward turn in life expectancy for blacks, ran through the standard list of hypotheses why the black community is so depressed. Then it said experts are persuaded "that there must be other reasons."[22] The article took several guesses for the reasons, but I would not be at all surprised to discover the basic problem is spiritual. It goes back to the shameful ways our Anglo-Americans have treated blacks in the past and at present. This sinful behavior has provided openings for high-ranking principalities and powers to establish spiritual strongholds that will not be loosened other than through corporate humility and repentance. I am aware of some who have begun this, but much more is needed.

How can this be done? John Dawson tells of his ministry in South Africa. He was convinced, "Apartheid is a spirit, not just a political phenomenon. It is a spirit that goes deep into African colonial history, with its roots in idolatry." So he preached on the sin of unrighteous judgment, led the large multiracial group in repentance of racial stereotypes and prejudice, then challenged each one in the audience to wash the feet of someone of another race. "Thousands of Afrikaners, Zulus, Indians, English, and Colored wept in each other's arms as a spirit of reconciliation spread."[23]

E. God's Plan of Attack and Timing

A great danger, which is all too common, is to go into spiritual warfare in the flesh. It is essential to hear from God what He wants us to do, how He wants us to do it, and when it should be done. This comes through serious prayer. This is where the prophetic dimension of the ministry of intercession is extremely important. Some of the possible consequences of missing God's plan of attack and timing are explained in the next chapter.

In summary, do not attempt strategic-level spiritual warfare without following these six rules. Be informed. Find out what many people are saying. I suggest you secure and study two other excellent lists of rules: Cindy Jacob's list in *Possessing the Gates of the Enemy* (pp. 242-245) and John Dawson's list in *Taking Our Cities for God* (pp. 163-219). Let's be wise and strong in the power of God's might.

■ REFLECTION QUESTIONS ■

1. Can you name any cities that have significant ongoing city-wide prayer efforts? Do you think one for your city would be feasible?

2. Discuss what is meant by affirming that pastors are the "spiritual gatekeepers" of a city.

3. How is the spiritual gift of intercession different from the expectation that all Christians should be praying people? Name some you know who might have this gift.

4. What do you think might be the "redemptive gift" or "redemptive purpose" of your city or town?

5. What would be some of the first steps in researching the spiritual history of your city?

Notes
1. John Dawson, *Taking Our Cities for God* (Lake Mary, FL: Creation House, 1989), p. 36.
2. Floyd McClung, *Seeing the City with the Eyes of God* (Tarrytown, NY: Chosen Books, 1991), p. 9.
3. Roger Greenway, "Book Review," *Evangelical Missions Quarterly,* October 1991, p. 430.
4. Dawson, *Taking Our Cities,* p. 36.
5. John Huffman, "New Prayer Program Tested in Costa Rica," *Prayer Pacesetters Sourcebook,* David Bryant, ed. (Concerts of Prayer International, Box 36008, Minneapolis, MN 55435, 1989), pp. 252-253.
6. Ibid., p. 253.
7. *The Bernal Report,* December 1989, p. 2.
8. Francis Frangipane, *The House of the Lord* (Lake Mary, FL: Creation House, 1991), p. 146.
9. Edgardo Silvoso in the brochure announcing *The First Annual Harvest Evangelism International Institute,* October 10-18, 1991, p. 2.
10. Dick Bernal, *Curses: What They Are and How to Break Them* (Companion Press, P.O. Box 351, Shippensburg, PA 17257-0351), pp. 71-84.
11. Laura Myers, "Christians Pray for San Francisco Souls," *Antelope Valley Press,* November 1, 1990, p. B3.
12. John Wimber, "Facing the '90s," *Equipping the Saints,* Summer 1989, p. 22.
13. Richard C. Lockwood, personal correspondence, April 16, 1990.
14. Kjell and Lena Sjöberg, *Newsletter,* March 6, 1991, pp. 2-3.
15. C. Peter Wagner, *Your Spiritual Gifts Can Help Your Church Grow* (Ventura, CA: Regal Books, 1979), p. 263.
16. Cindy Jacobs, *Possessing the Gates of the Enemy* (Tarrytown, NY: Chosen Books, 1991), p. 56.
17. Dawson, *Taking Our Cities,* p. 39.
18. Ibid., p. 44.
19. McClung, *Seeing the City,* p. 34.
20. Ibid.
21. Koji Honda, "An Apology to the Peoples of Asia," *Japan Update, Bulletin of the Japan Evangelical Association,* October 1990, p. 8.
22. "Perils of Being Born Black," *Time,* December 10, 1990, p. 78.
23. John Dawson, "Seventh Time Around," *Engaging the Enemy,* C. Peter Wagner, ed. (Ventura, CA: Regal Books, 1991), pp. 137-138.

Avoiding the Pitfalls

CHAPTER TEN

S TRATEGIC-LEVEL SPIRITUAL WARFARE IS NOT FOR EVERY-one. I was told that fighter pilots in the Persian Gulf War were under constant scrutiny for symptoms of fear. If any showed up, even to the slightest degree, they were immediately pulled out of the conflict and sent back home. Likewise, doing battle against the spiritual principalities and powers is not an activity for the timid or the fainthearted. It is war, and casualties are to be expected. I know very few, if any, veterans of strategic-level spiritual warfare who cannot tell stories of how they have been wounded in one way or another.

CASUALTIES OF THE WAR

Doris and I began going out to the front lines in Argentina in 1990. Within months, we had the worst family fight in 40 years of marriage, we had a severe problem with one of our closest intercessors, and Doris was incapacitated for almost 5 months with blown-out disks, back surgery and knee surgery. There is no question at all in our minds, or in those of the people who pray for us, that this was a direct backlash from the spirits who were so riled up by our invading their territory.

One of the most experienced spiritual warriors in our nation is my good friend Larry Lea. As I have mentioned previously, a great public victory came with his San Francisco Halloween Breakthrough in 1990. Yet, the enemy managed to put Larry's name on the casualty list as well. The next four months were some of the worst in his life. He needed surgery for a hernia. He had a severe problem with one of his closest intercessors. The finances of his ministry dropped to such a low level it was frightening. His father died of cancer. And other things so bizarre happened that they should not be mentioned. He even wondered if he should continue his ministry.

Although I do not believe we can totally avoid the kind of casualties Larry Lea and I experienced, I believe we can minimize them as we learn more about strategic-level spiritual warfare. America was amazed at the relatively few casualties in the Persian Gulf War. I hope we learn how to do spiritual warfare as well and that we see the frequency and severity of the casualties significantly reduced.

LEARNING FROM MISTAKES

Nothing is wrong with making mistakes or failing. I don't mind failing as long as I keep my long-range vision, regroup after the failure, learn from my mistakes, move ahead once again and avoid making the same mistake twice.

I will never forget when Doris and I first met Pablo Bottari, whom I mentioned in chapter 1 as the leader of the deliverance ministries in Carlos Annacondia's citywide crusades in Argentina. He was giving us a private tour of the "spiritual intensive care unit" tent, which he supervises. We asked him how he learned to do this unusual kind of ministry. He said, "Do you want to know? We learned by making every mistake we could possibly make!" Then, among other things, he told us the story of the "Demon of Keys."

The "Demon of Keys"
It seems that a man was standing in the crowd attending one of Carlos Annacondia's crusades. One of the interesting features of

---

If we go into spiritual warfare and expect to have God's power without humility on our part we are in trouble.

---

these crusades is that they are held in vacant lots and no chairs are used (except a few up front for the sick and elderly). On an average night, between 5,000 and 20,000 will be standing in dirt, often covered with some grass and weeds, from 8:00 to 11:00 P.M. The lighting is adequate, but not excellent.

This night Annacondia began his usual public rebuke of the evil spirits. The evil spirits started manifesting, demonized people fell to the ground, and the specially trained ministry team called "stretcher bearers" started picking them up, half carrying and half dragging them into the deliverance tent. Our friend stood there watching the activities when his keys fell out of his hand into the grass and weeds on the ground. The poor man bent over, and because the light was so poor, began groping around searching for his keys. A team of stretcher bearers spotted him and assumed that he, too, was demonized. Before the spectator knew what was happening, they had gripped his arms and were pulling him away.

"The keys! The keys!" he shouted, but to no avail. When he got into the deliverance tent the stretcher bearers announced that he was being attacked by a demon of keys! Pablo Bottari never did tell us whether the man ever got back his keys.

TEN PITFALLS TO AVOID

Pablo Bottari and the rest of us have made many mistakes. No doubt we will continue to make them, but hopefully they will become fewer and fewer as time goes by. Here is a list of common pitfalls of strategic-level spiritual warfare we need to be aware of and avoid to the degree possible.

1. Ignorance

Ignorance is first on my list of pitfalls because it is undoubtedly the most effective tool of the enemy. It works in several ways.

Many Christians are ignorant of spiritual warfare in general, and even among those who do know about spiritual warfare many are unaware of the strategic-level variety that deals with territorial spirits. Those who do not know a war is on pose no threat to Satan and the forces of darkness.

Some who are aware of strategic-level spiritual warfare and do not deny the existence of principalities and powers, have decided it is not an activity intended for the church today because they have never taken the pains to investigate it deeply enough. They think it has insufficient theological, biblical and experiential ground. They have decided not to enlist in the army.

Others have a desire to do damage to the spiritual strongholds over a city or nation, but are ignorant of sound methodology. Fortunately, resources and teaching in this field are multiplying rapidly and this type of ignorance should soon be a thing of the past.

One of the worst dangers is to become involved in strategic-level spiritual warfare without knowing you are in it. I will not mention the name of the denomination, but a group of American Christian young people who were opposed to pornography decided to attend the Porno Festival in Copenhagen, Denmark, with the express purpose of denouncing pornography as sin and calling the people there to repentance. Eighteen of them went and preached day after day in front of porno stores and displays. They reported hundreds of conversions, although further investigation showed that little or none of that fruit actually remained. But the worst thing was that within the next few years, every single one of the 18 fell into pornography addiction or illicit sex!

The danger is that ignorance of the spirit world can lead to foolishness. These young people had no idea they were not wrestling with flesh and blood, but against principalities and powers, and they paid the consequences.

2. Fear

Many Christian leaders are inwardly fearful of engaging the enemy on the higher levels. They hear what happened to the likes of Doris Wagner after warfare in Argentina, or Larry Lea after San Francisco, and they decide they don't want that sort of thing happening to them. The fear is rarely expressed openly because there is good reason not to admit it.

First, these leaders are well aware that Jesus has defeated the enemy once for all as I have mentioned many times previously, and they know they need not doubt who will win the war.

Secondly, they believe that perfect love casts out all fear and "He who fears has not been made perfect in love" (1 John 4:18). Admitting fear could be regarded as admitting a lack of love, and that is something few leaders are prepared to do.

One leader who did admit his fear is Floyd McClung of Youth With a Mission. He tells how he used to evade questions concerning the devil by saying, "Satan loves sin, fear, and atten-tion. I will not give him any of the three." But then after doing this once too often, the Holy Spirit convicted him and he hum-bled himself before the Lord. God spoke to him inwardly say-ing, "I am disappointed in your response. You have little knowledge of the demonic realm and no authority over Satan as did my disciples many years ago. Your answer reflected your own fears."

This word from the Lord turned him around. He confessed that he was responding to the questions in fear, "a well-dis-guised fear dressed up in theological terms, but fear nonethe-less. I may have fooled some people, but not the Lord." What was McClung's problem? "I was afraid of extremism. I was afraid of the unknown."[1]

During the Middle East crisis of the early 1990s, some Amer-icans formed "anti-war movements" in an attempt to break the nation's determination to carry out a just war. Rick Joyner sees a similar phenomenon among Christian leaders. He says, "There is a very subtle spiritual anti-war movement that the enemy would use to derail the church's resolve in spiritual warfare." In Joyner's opinion, "The spiritual anti-war movement is rooted in idealism and is combined with a subtle fear of the enemy."[2]

Although we should respect the power of the enemy, we should not fear it. This leads me to the next pitfall.

3. Underestimating the Enemy

I happen to be a dairy farmer. This is the vocation I learned as a child, and I even have my B.S. degree in dairy production. Most of my experience came in the days before artificial insem-ination when dairy bulls were very much a part of farm life. Many people do not know that dairy bulls (unlike beef bulls) are one of the most vicious animals known. Like the devil, they are extremely powerful and they are extremely mean. Give them the slightest opportunity and they will kill you. In dairy country like mine in upstate New York, every town has its stories of those who were seriously wounded or killed by bulls.

One of the reasons I was never the victim of a bull's attack is that I so greatly respect them. I know what they can do, when they do it and how they do it. But I am not afraid of them. I can make a dairy bull do nearly anything I want him to do. My power doesn't even compare to that of a bull, but I can lead one into the show ring, for example, just like a little kitten.

Satan and his forces are like the bull. Martin Luther said, "On earth is not his equal." But through the blood of Jesus Christ and the weapons of our spiritual warfare we need not be afraid. Even so, the minute you underestimate Satan's power and lose your respect for him, you can be dead.

Some, I am sad to report, have actually lost their lives in strategic-level spiritual warfare. One of my Fuller students, Wilson Awasu of Ghana, wrote a research paper describing a Presbyterian pastor, C. Y. Adjanku, who ordered a tree enshrined by satanic priests to be cut down. When the tree fell, he dropped dead.

Among the most highly respected intercessors and spiritual warriors today is Johannes Facius of Germany, coordinator of Intercessors International. I point this out so that we understand we are not talking about a novice, but a veteran. He tells how back in 1986, a team of intercessors went to the Soviet Union and entered the Lenin Mausoleum in Moscow. They felt they should pronounce judgment upon the "god of the Soviet system," Vladimir Lenin.

What happened in the heavenlies at that time we do not know. We do know that Soviet Communism soon crumbled. But Facius says, "It was through this move against the Enemy that I suffered one of the strangest attacks of sickness that I have ever experienced." The initial attack lasted one day, but soon afterward came a debilitating heart disease. He sees it as a counterattack of the spirit of death they had resisted in the Lenin Mausoleum. Three years of severe depression followed.

After that he was delivered in a session that lasted less than 30 seconds![3]

When Facius mentioned the spirit of death I shuddered, because Doris and I are convinced that the perpetrator of the attacks on her was the spirit of death from Resistencia, Argentina: San La Muerte.

4. Spiritual Arrogance

If we go into spiritual warfare and expect to have God's power without humility on our part we are in trouble. Paul said to the Corinthians, "I was with you in weakness, in fear, and in much trembling" (1 Cor. 2:3) and, "When I am weak, then I am strong" (2 Cor. 12:10). At the same time, Paul was one of the most powerful spiritual warriors in the New Testament. He made even Diana of the Ephesians tremble! Effective spiritual warfare requires a delicate balance of weakness and power. The minute we begin to think we are doing it ourselves we become vulnerable to the enemy's attack.

Johannes Facius admits this was part of his problem. He knew he was to stay in unbroken, intimate fellowship with the Lord. But he let it slip. Facius says, "Due to too much busyness—busyness in the Lord's business—I came to the point where I let go of my dependency on the Lord."[4]

5. Lack of Personal Intercession

I believe intercession for Christian leaders is the most under-utilized source of spiritual power in our churches today. In fact, my next book in this series is projected to be on that subject.

My advice is that no one should become involved in strategic-level spiritual warfare without definite assurance of being covered with intercessory prayer. In the famous spiritual warfare passage in Ephesians 6, the apostle Paul himself begged the Ephesians to intercede for him (see Eph. 6:19). He asked the Colossians for the same thing (see Col. 4:3).

The forces of darkness certainly are all too aware of the power released through intercessors as leaders minister in spiritual warfare. Within a period of just a few months, for example, I witnessed three leaders in the area of spiritual warfare, all members of the Spiritual Warfare Network, lose their number one intercessor: Larry Lea, Peter Wagner and Edgardo Silvoso. Each case happened under different circumstances, so Satan varies his tactics. I began the chapter by mentioning Larry Lea

---

I believe intercession for Christian leaders is the most underutilized source of spiritual power in our churches today.

---

and me. Edgardo Silvoso's situation is a story in itself. I will disguise the names and places to avoid any undue embarrassment.

Silvoso's intercessor allowed jealousy to creep in when an outsider came into his area and led in some very powerful warfare praying. The intercessor, whom we'll call Henry, asked his roommate to go out into the city with him one night to war against the spirits—presumably to assure himself and his roommate that he also had spiritual power. When they got back to the hotel and went to bed, two women, one a blonde and one a brunette, entered their room and offered Henry his choice of one to sleep with. His roommate was sleeping. Henry jumped up and locked himself in the bathroom. The women left, and he went back to bed. Before he knew it, three women had come in, the same two with another. They said, "If you don't like us, why don't you sleep with her?" Henry got up and ran outside the room.

When Henry returned, the women were gone, but his roommate woke up choking and totally covered with perspiration.

His breath was almost gone, and they feared he would die. They prayed, and the attack lifted.

The next night Henry was driving the van to the city where he lived, moving at a high speed. Suddenly his body became paralyzed from the waist down, he choked as if there were hands around his throat, and the van veered off the highway. He could only yell to the other passengers, "Please pray!" The van miraculously stayed upright, came to a stop, and no one was hurt. Later they learned that at that very instant the person he had become jealous of, along with two companions, had heard from God that He wanted them to pray for Henry. They prayed fervently, and God answered!

The good news is they weren't hurt.

The bad news is that Henry, who previously was known as a powerful intercessor, has not been able to pray well ever since. Hopefully, this will turn out to be a temporary situation as was the case with Johannes Facius. Facius also admits this was one of his problems.

Facius says, "Like the apostle Paul, we need to ask for the covering of prayers from fellow believers. I failed here. We need to mobilize prayer partners for every strategic and warring action we undertake."[5]

6. Unguided Prayer

I have mentioned several times that intimacy with the Father through prayer and seeing clearly what the Father is doing is crucial for effective warfare praying. Without this our prayers can be unguided, and therefore weak. Wesley Duewel says, "When you confine your intercession to your own understanding, you not only may miss God's intent but may hinder His plan. Wait on God until He confirms His will to you."[6] This, of course, requires listening to God in prayer.

I like the story Duewel tells about Mrs. Ed Spahr, an intercessor who was awakened in the night to pray for Jerry Rose, a missionary in Irian Jaya. This was so clear and at such a specific time that she wrote to Jerry Rose the next day and told him about it. Four other letters arrived from prayer partners telling him that God had them praying at exactly the same time. At the time all five were praying, Rose was standing with his arms tied behind his back and a Stone Age savage was preparing to thrust a spear through his body! But before he could do it, another man from the tribe stepped up, said something to the spearman, and they immediately released Jerry!

This is an example of guided prayer, the kind of prayer that moves the forces of darkness.[7]

7. Poor Timing

One of the local pastors working with me in the Pasadena for Christ project is my friend, Che Ahn. He told me how his church went through a very significant month of prayer and fasting not long ago. One of the many things they received from God that month was the revelation that some of the most powerful territorial spirits over Pasadena were centered in City Hall. So they gathered a team of 30 one evening and went to City Hall to tear down strongholds.

They had not prayed long when they realized they were in high-level warfare. The counterattack came. When Che got home that night he suffered the most severe attack of hay fever he had experienced since he was a child. His children began having nightmares every night. They dreamed of horrors such as people being decapitated, limbs torn off and their father being murdered. Che explained that since they have no television his children would have no way of being mentally programmed with such things in the natural. It had to be spiritual.

As we talked we agreed that although the revelation had undoubtedly been accurate, the timing of the public warfare might have been off. It may not have been God's *kairos* or strategic time for the encounter to take place.

In the neighboring city of Monrovia, a similar incident took place where the timing was not right. Leigh Jackson, an intercessor, had been burdened to start a prayer movement for her city in 1985. In April of 1988, after other successful prayer meetings, she called together the pastors of the city to pray within the council chambers of the City Hall. Much to her consternation, one of the pastors usurped control of the meeting and turned it in a direction contrary to the vision she had received. Leigh, as a woman, didn't feel she could exercise authority and do anything about it. The prayer movement stalled.

She tried it again in 1989, and this also turned out to be a false start. It wasn't until late 1990 when she finally heard from God about the timing, and at this writing the prayer movement is getting underway as she hoped.

Many of us, including me, have a tendency to be impatient. Once we know what needs to be done, we want to get it done now. But if we get ahead of God we might as well forget about anything significant happening because it will be done in the flesh and not in the Spirit.

8. Empty Rhetoric

One of my concerns is that some will become interested in strategic-level spiritual warfare, but do it so unwisely that their excessive praying turns out to be nothing but empty rhetoric. Instead of pushing back the forces of darkness, they are only making noise.

Some of the authors in the field of warfare praying share prayers they have used and found effective. These are good prayers, and nothing is wrong with using similar prayers over and over again. Those from liturgical traditions find that great spiritual power can be released through using prayers written by others.

However, the danger needs to be recognized that some rather immature believers can fall into the trap of using the prayers of others as if they were magical formulas. If they just say the right words and shout them loud enough, Satan will be defeated. If a prayer works for Dick Bernal or Tom White or Gwen Shaw, it will work for me.

I do not believe that empty rhetoric is one of the worst or most dangerous pitfalls. In most cases nothing happens, because neither God nor the principalities pay much attention to it. When it is done, everything is much the same as it was before. But the danger comes when the person who prays thinks that something happens in the heavenlies and acts on that assumption. Declaring victory when there is no victory can have serious consequences. This is what the Argentina military leaders attempted in the Falkland Islands War and as a result they severely traumatized the social psychology of the entire nation.

When many serious, thinking Christians see foolishness disguised as spiritual warfare in churches or on television they reject the whole idea. This is the point at which Satan can gain a victory through empty rhetoric.

9. No Covering

If reading a book like this excites you, and if you want to enlist in the army of God for strategic-level spiritual warfare, do not do it under any circumstances without the covering of your spiritual superiors. Your pastor or the elders of your church are agents of God appointed to oversee your spiritual welfare. You leave yourself vulnerable and open to severe attack if you do not have this spiritual covering.

By this I do not mean your pastor will necessarily need to join you in the hands-on warfare. But he or she needs to give you an explicit blessing in one form or another.

For most this is a simple principle to apply. However, for the top levels of Christian leadership it becomes more complex. Who pastors the pastor? This has been a personal problem for me over the years, because the church I belong to is so large that the one who holds the title of senior pastor is usually too busy to give me and my family individual pastoral care. God brought this to my attention recently when I was reading what Johannes Facius said: "I believe that every one of us, including God's servants, needs a pastor." Then he mentions the name of the person who functions as his pastor even though he lives in a different country, Sven Nilsson of Sweden.[8]

Doris and I prayed about it and agreed to approach John Maxwell and his wife, Margaret, to see if they would be willing to carry this burden. They readily agreed, and I believe this relationship will continue for a long time. As my pastor, John now provides the covering and the spiritual authority I need for my ministry, even though his church, Skyline Wesleyan of San Diego, is more than 100 miles away.

10. Moving out Alone

Do not plan on or attempt to do strategic-level spiritual warfare alone. Always do it in a group. Jesus said He will be present where two or three are gathered. This is another way of saying there should be more than one. "If two lie down together, they will keep warm; but how can one be warm alone?" (Eccles. 4:11).

This was brought to my attention recently through a conversation I had with Alfred H. Ells, a Christian marriage counselor from Phoenix. He told me how he was driving his car in the city at Christmastime when he heard on the radio that the ACLU was requiring the city to take down the public Christmas decorations. He became angry, and in the car he began cursing out loud the spirit of ACLU. He immediately saw a vision of an ugly being, and felt a blow in his side. He turned and said, "What is that?" and then took a sharp blow just like a fist on the left side of his face. The pain was terrible. He could hardly open his mouth. Back in the office, some laid on hands and prayed and the pain left.

Later Alfred was praying about it and said to God, "What's going on?" God answered and said, "You had no business doing that!"

Looking back, we saw that Alfred Ells had violated several of the items on this list of pitfalls, and one of them was going at it alone.

HOW WARFARE PRAYER CAN WORK

One of the Bible's most dramatic examples of effective warfare prayer is Elijah coming against Baal. Baal was a classic territorial spirit, the principality over the Phoenicians and the Canaanites. What his exact boundaries were I do not know, but I do know he was not the spirit over, for example, China, Scandinavia, the Andes Indians or Australian Aborigines, all of which existed in those days.

Baal succeeded in capturing the allegiance of King Ahab, who married Jezebel, converted to Baal worship, and built a temple and an altar to that evil principality.

God raised up Elijah to lead the strategic-level spiritual warfare, and the story is found in 1 Kings 17—19. Elijah was not wrestling so much against flesh and blood (Jezebel and Ahab), but against principalities and powers (Baal and his forces of darkness). The climax of the story is a dramatic power encounter.

In preparation for the power encounter, Elijah publicly proclaimed a drought on the land. Through it, God sustained Elijah by bringing birds to feed him and by multiplying food at the widow's house. God reminded Elijah of His power by raising the widow's son from the dead.

Then the Lord's timing (the *kairos* moment) came for Baal to be defeated and the drought to end. Elijah announced it would rain and then openly challenged Baal through King Ahab. The events are well-known. Baal could not light the fire called down by his priests, but God did so even after the firewood had been soaked with water. This was such a public embarrassment that 450 of Baal's priests were executed. When the power of that territorial spirit was broken, the rain came!

But the counterattack came also. Jezebel was furious. Elijah, weakened by the warfare, fled. God sent an angel to feed him, but he went into a period of severe depression. God met him and spoke to him in a still, small voice and told him there were still 7,000 followers of Jehovah.

A Glorious Finale

Then God gave Elijah a glorious finale:
- He anointed a new king,
- He identified his replacement, Elisha,
- Elijah was taken to heaven in a chariot of fire. And, along with Moses, he was one of two people from the past chosen to join Jesus on the Mount of Transfiguration! What a reward for the faithful warrior!

But where does *warfare prayer* enter the picture? Nothing in 1 Kings says that Elijah prayed.

God did not want to leave us wondering whether Elijah prayed or not. Through James He informs us that Elijah's major spiritual weapon was the same as ours: *warfare prayer.* "Elijah was a man with a nature like ours, and he prayed earnestly that it would not rain; and it did not rain on the land for three years and six months. And he prayed again, and the heaven gave rain, and the earth produced its fruit" (Jas. 5:17,18).

In what context does James mention this prayer, which we know to be warfare prayer from 1 Kings? James uses it as an illustration of the principle: "The effective, fervent prayer of a righteous man avails much" (Jas. 5:16).

This biblical illustration shows that God has been and is calling His people to warfare prayer.

"He who has an ear, let him hear what the Spirit says to the churches" (Rev. 2:7).

▬ REFLECTION QUESTIONS ▬

1. Why is it that some Christians are fearful of dealing with the spirit world even if they know that Jesus is on their side?
2. If personal intercession is so important for Christian leaders to receive so that they will not turn out to be casualties, why is it so rare?
3. How can we be sure that what we are praying for is the will of God at a particular time?
4. Suppose we fall into any of the pitfalls mentioned in this chapter. Will God always overrule, or is the danger real?
5. Pray with others around you that God will show you and your friends specifically what steps you should take to implement what you have learned by reading this book.

Notes

1. Floyd McClung, *Seeing Our Cities with the Eyes of God* (Tarrytown, NY: Chosen Books, 1991), p. 18.
2. Rick Joyner, "The Spiritual Meaning of the Persian Gulf War," *The Morning Star Prophetic Bulletin*, February 15, 1991, p. 1.
3. Johannes Facius, "Let God Be God," *Intercessors for America Newsletter*, March 1991, p. 3. This revealing and instructive story of Johannes Facius is told in detail in his book, *God Can Do It Without Me!* (Chichester, England, Sovereign World Books, 1990).
4. Ibid.
5. Ibid.
6. Wesley L. Duewel, *Mighty Prevailing Prayer* (Grand Rapids, MI: Francis Asbury Press of Zondervan Publishing House, 1990), p. 258.
7. Ibid., p. 260.
8. Facius, "Let God Be God," p. 3.

Index

spiritism, 24, 173
spiritual arrogance, 188
spiritual boot camp, 105-107
spiritual discernment, 148
spiritual factors, 46-47
spiritual gatekeepers, 179
spiritual leadership, 121-122
spiritual mapping, 46, 63, 100, 150-158, 165, 172, 175
spiritual unity, 167-168
spiritual warfare, casualties in, 182
spiritual warfare, dangers in, 181-197
spiritual warfare, fear of, 185-186
spiritual warfare, ground-level, 16-17
Spiritual Warfare Network, 45
spiritual warfare, occult-level, 17-18
spiritual warfare, public, 31-33
spiritual warfare, strategic-level, 18-19
spiritual warfare, three levels, 16-19
spiritual warfare, timing for, 178, 191-192
spirituality, 11
Stacey, Vivienne, 84, 86
Sterk, Vernon J., 100-101, 103, 147, 149, 159
Strang, Stephen, 34
strategic-level intercession, 12
strategic-level intercession, rhetoric in, 192-193
strategic-level intercession, shouting in, 193
strongholds, demonic, 30, 64-65, 129-131, 175-176
strongman, 60-61
Stutzman, Ervin R., 80, 86
submit to God, 108-109
Succoth Benoth, 93
succubus, 87
Sun Goddess of Japan, 134, 140
superstition, 74
Synan, Vinson, 114
Syria, 91-92
Tagore, Rabindranath, 143
Taking Our Cities for God, 46, 132, 141, 153, 160, 161, 178, 179
Talbot School of Theology, 68, 97
Taoism, 151
Tartak, 93
10/40 Window, 151-152
territorial spirits, 13, 18-19, 22, 45-46, 65, 85, 87-102, 129-131, 144-148, 176
territoriality, spiritual, 12, 87-102
Thailand, 75-76
theological seminaries, 11
Thornburgh, Attorney General Dick, 138
timing for warfare, 191-192
traditional evangelicals, 48
truth encounter, 64-65
Tzotzil Indians, 100-101, 147, 149

underestimating the enemy, 186-188
unity, spiritual, 167-168
unreached peoples, 162
urban evangelism, 26, 60, 161-179
urban ministry, 161-179
urban mission, 161-179
Uruguay, 23, 29
Venezuela, 23
violence, spirit of, 145, 147
visible and invisible, 139-140, 151, 152
Vision of the Future Church, 13
voodoo, 43
Wagner, C. Peter, 34, 70, 86, 102-103, 170, 179, 189
Wagner, Doris, 15, 28, 31-33, 42, 43, 81-82, 85, 86, 110, 117, 135, 163, 164, 171, 181-182, 185, 188, 194
Wagner, Ruth, 110
Walsh, James, 159
warfare prayer, 12, 14, 20, 27-28, 33, 37, 43, 48, 60, 66, 81, 96, 145, 162, 163
Warkentin, Irene, 83, 85
Warkentin, Kevin, 83
warlocks, 17
Warner, Timothy, 46, 62, 70
water devil, 73-75, 85
Webb, Leland, 80, 86
White, John, 21
White, Tom, 45, 46, 127, 141, 153, 154, 160, 193
wicca, 170
wilderness, 53
Williams, Don, 91, 102
Wimber, John, 11, 39, 40, 109, 124, 172, 179
Wink, Walter, 11, 64, 70, 95-96, 102, 123, 124, 150
witchcraft, 24, 33, 92, 130, 171
witchcraft, spirit of, 32, 145, 147, 156
witches, 13, 17-18
Woodberry, J. Dudley, 86
World Vision International, 144
worldview, 99
Wormwood, 146, 147
worship, 48
Wray, Daniel E., 34
Wrestling with Dark Angels, 11
Wycliffe Bible Translators, 13-14
Yajval Balamil, 100
Yoder, John Howard, 95
Yoshiyama, Hiroshi, 138
Your Spiritual Gifts Can Help Your Church Grow, 174, 179
Youth With a Mission, 132, 185
Zimbabwe, 100
Zinacanteco Indians, 101
zodiac, signs of, 98